CHRISTIAN BELIEF

CHRISTIAN BELIEF

★

A COURSE
OF OPEN LECTURES DELIVERED
IN THE UNIVERSITY
OF CAMBRIDGE

BY

ALEC R. VIDLER

SCM PRESS LTD
BLOOMSBURY STREET, LONDON

First published April 1950
Reprinted December 1950
Reprinted February 1954
Cheap edition November 1957

Printed in Great Britain by Staples Printers Limited
at their Rochester, Kent, establishment

CONTENTS

★

PREFACE

*

This course of open lectures was delivered, at the invitation of the Board of the Divinity Faculty, in the University of Cambridge during the Michaelmas term, 1949. The lectures are printed as they were delivered, with only a few slight modifications. References in the notes indicate some of my debts. A man who lectures on a subject of this kind is not in a position to measure or record all his debts.

A. R. V.

The Cloisters,
  Windsor Castle

I

BELIEF IN GOD

*

W HEN I was invited to give this course of lectures it was suggested that I should take 'Christian Belief' as the subject. We have heard a good deal in recent years about the application of the Christian Faith to politics and social problems and this and that, but there comes a time when men reasonably ask just what is this Christian Faith that we are talking about. My aim, therefore, will be to give as clear and faithful an explanation as I can of the main Christian doctrines. I am not here to do 'Christian propaganda'. There is a proper time and place for that, although the word 'propaganda' has for too familiar reasons acquired a bad meaning, and there is certainly such a thing as *bad* Christian propaganda. I design not to play upon your emotions nor to dazzle you with dialectical fireworks, but to offer you trustworthy information about the Christian Faith so that you will be in a better position to make your own judgment about its truth. At the same time, I cannot, nor do I wish to disguise the fact that if you judge what I say to be true it will not leave your life unaffected. The subject, I mean, is one that is liable to move you 'to do something about it'.

This would not be the case with other subjects on which I might lecture. For instance, it happens that one of my hobbies is collecting wild bees—or *hymenoptra aculeata*, to dignify them with their Latin title. It is possible that, if I knew more about these remarkable insects than I do as yet, I might be able to produce an interesting lecture about them. But while in that event I might hope to provide you with an hour's distracting and even instructive entertainment, I should not expect you to do anything about it. There would be no reason why you should do anything about it; you probably have already more than enough hobbies of your own.

Christianity, however, is not a hobby—although you might be

9

pardoned if you supposed that it was, since many professing Christians appear to regard it as little more than that. Christianity —to use for the present a word for which I hold no brief, and shall shortly discard—Christianity is, to say the least, a world-view which claims to be true for all men, and a way of life which claims to be valid for all men. Either it is true for all men, whether they know it or not; or it is true for no one, not even for those people who are under the illusion that it is true. You cannot listen to a course of lectures about it without giving your verdict that it is true or false, for to withhold a verdict is to reject its claim to be true for you. Nevertheless, it is not my business here to press you for a verdict, as it would be if I were preaching a course of sermons, so that I shall labour the point no further.

I propose to-day first to call your attention to a number of other points which you ought to bear in mind in considering Christian belief, and then to make a beginning with the subject of belief in God; the whole course of lectures will, I hope, be about that.

The first point is that you will hardly make anything of Christian belief unless you recognize that to exist as a human being is to be surrounded by mystery. 'The highest knowledge', Albert Schweitzer has said, 'is to know that we are surrounded by mystery'.[1] I am using the word 'mystery' here, not in the sense of an interesting possibility, but of an incomprehensible reality. I do not say that to exist is to be completely enveloped in mystery, for that is not the case. There are many things which are, as we say, matters of plain common sense. There are some things like the *simpler* elements of mathematics which are clear to anyone whose powers of thinking have been quite moderately developed. What is more important, there is a great deal in the existing world, which was previously regarded as mysterious or which had previously not even been surmised, that has become tolerably clear to anyone who is prepared to read, mark, learn, and inwardly digest the illuminating deliverances of the various sciences which have made such prodigious advances during the last hundred years. You will not hear from me any of those crabbing or belittling observations which some, at any rate, of the camp-followers of theology, prompted, I suppose, by jealousy or fear, are wont to make about the magnificent achievements of the natural and human sciences. It must be confessed that during this period theology has not made comparable advances; partly no doubt because nothing like the same amount of hard work, patient research, open-minded investigation, and disinterested devotion has been expended on it. Theology is not at present in a position to throw its weight about, and it makes itself ridiculous when it says, as an English Roman Catholic bishop said a year or two ago, 'We have the assurance of our position. We have the certainty of the possession of truth. We have the answers to all the questions' (sic).[2]

If you are looking for dogmatism of that kind, I have none to offer you. I hold that, when account is taken of all that is known or that is scientifically knowable, there still remain mysterious depths in the whole universe and in human existence which mortal man has not fathomed and which there is no reason to suppose he is capable of completely fathoming, if by fathoming we mean clearing up and mastering once and for all. Professor Paul Tillich has told how he was sitting under a tree with a great biologist. Suddenly the biologist exclaimed: 'I would like to know something about this tree!' He, of course, knew everything that science had to say about it. Tillich asked him what he meant. And he answered: 'I want to know what this tree means for itself. I want to understand the life of this tree. It is so strange, so unapproachable.'[3] Tillich gives another illustration of the same point. 'A Chinese emperor asked a famous painter to paint a picture of a rooster for him. The painter assented, but said it would take a long time. After a year the emperor reminded him of his promise. The painter replied that after a year of studying the rooster he had just begun to perceive the surface of its nature. After another year the artist asserted that he had just begun to penetrate the essence of this kind of life. And so on, year after year. Finally, after ten years of concentration on the nature of the rooster, he painted the picture—a work described as an inexhaustible revelation of the divine ground of the universe in one small part of it.'[4] A fortiori there are unfathomed and inexhaustible depths in human existence and in human history. If you did not at any rate suspect that this may be so, you would not be here. And that is what I mean when I say that you will hardly make anything of Christian belief unless you recognize that to exist as a human being is to be surrounded by mystery. If Christian belief does anything, it casts some light on those mysterious depths, or rather testifies to the shining of some light out of those mysterious depths. It testifies to the shining of sufficient light to draw men to go on seeking, of sufficient light to direct and keep men in the way of finding. As a (neglected) French theologian has said, Christian faith 'does not mean being settled in prejudiced adherence to the abstract formulas of a creed; it is a ceaseless striving after renewal, a continuous search. . . . The truth for us is not a terminus: it is the way that we have to follow.' [5]

This leads me to the second point. Christian belief is not a finished or rounded-off system of doctrines such as could be learned off out of a text-book and from which the correct party-line on every question that arises in heaven or on earth can be deduced. Christian belief springs indeed from the conviction that a light is constantly shining upon our way and that once upon a time the very Light of the World became manifest in the thick of our strange history. But very much remains dark to our mortal eyes and hidden from our finite minds. 'We must, for the sake of our own inner integrity, be true to our darkness as well as to our light.' [6] It has been easy for Christians as well as for other people to forget this. Vanity is always moving us to claim to know more than we do or can know. 'As soon as we start to explain anything, it is difficult for our limited minds not to substitute what is easy to understand for the fullness of experience'; [7] so we deceive ourselves that we have understood more than we have in fact. Those of you who study ancient literary texts, in which it is often doubtful what the author actually wrote, will be acquainted with the maxim, *lectio difficilior potius*, the more difficult reading is to be preferred; and that maxim holds good on a larger field. In trying to read the mysteries of existence, we are always tempted to prefer the easier reading, the simpler solution. But we shall be wise if we especially distrust simple solutions of old problems, and the cocksureness of upstart pseudo-philosophers. We must always be seeking to understand more, but it is folly to suppose that we shall ever succeed in tidying up the whole universe and in neatly arranging its exhibits like a Natural History Museum.

Katherine Mansfield happily compared that type of mind, 'cultivated minds', to cultivated gardens. 'Such a type of mind doesn't really attract me (she said). I admire it, I appreciate all *les soins et les peines* that have gone to produce it—but it leaves me cold. After all, the adventure is over. There is now nothing to do but to trim and to lop and to keep back—all faintly depressing labours. No, no, the mind I love must still have wild places, a tangled orchard where dark damsons drop in the heavy grass, an overgrown little wood, the chance of a snake or two (real snakes), a pool that nobody's fathomed the depths of—and paths threaded with those little flowers planted by the mind. It must have *real* hiding places, not artificial ones—not gazebos and mazes. And I have never yet met the cultivated mind that has not had its shrubbery. I loathe and detest shrubberies.' [8] Christian belief is not like a cultivated garden; and cultivated minds in that sense are a menace to the growth of theological insight.

My third point is that the grounds for believing in God, in Christ, in the Holy Spirit, cannot, as I see the state of the case, be put into the form of a compelling argument from which there is no possibility of escape. I do not say this in order to suggest that Christian belief should be allowed to pass, and can be accepted, after a less rigorous intellectual examination than other forms of belief. By no means. No belief about the nature of the world, no interpretation of all the facts of existence, is intellectually compelling or demonstrative. There are difficulties and unresolved enigmas in every great creed. Only with the little, shallow creeds is it otherwise. A man can secure complete intellectual satisfaction or logical coherence in his system of belief only if he glosses over, brushes aside or explains away those facts which embarrass the system of his choice and cannot be fitted into it. This is commonly enough done, and anyone who is disposed to be an ostrich may be as dogmatic as he pleases. The most that can be claimed for Christian belief, the most that can be claimed for any creed that is determined to reckon fully with all the evidences, conflicting and bewildering as they are, is that it accounts more adequately for all the facts than any alternative, and leaves fewer difficulties jutting out. Probability is the guide of life, and the most confident faith (whether Christian or any other) when it is intellectually considered, is found to rest at most on a very high degree of probability. This is so, not only with belief in God, but with our commonest and most familiar actions and attitudes. They cannot be intellectually justified up to the hilt and freed from every possibility of sceptical cavil. The worst of sceptics is that they are not sceptical enough. It has often been remarked, but it is less often remembered, that there are baffling philosophical problems concerning things we confidently do every day. As Lord Balfour said, 'Perhaps the enlightened lounger, requesting a club-waiter to shut the window, brushes aside, or ignores, as many philosophic puzzles as a mother passionately praying for the safety of her child.' [9] These puzzles need not, and do not, inhibit us from asking a waiter to shut the window, and likewise it is quite consistent with confident belief in God and with honest prayer to confess the persistence of outstanding intellectual difficulties.

No one has insisted more firmly than Dr. Tennant on the distinction between logical certainty and practical certitude. 'Certitude', as Newman said, 'is a mental state; certainty is a quality of propositions.' [10] It may be impossible for a philosophical sceptic to demonstrate to the satisfaction of himself and his colleagues that his wife exists; all the same he is in practice sure that she does exist. Likewise it is possible for a man to believe in God and to trust him unreservedly, even while he admits that he cannot produce a completely conclusive argument that God exists.

The truth is in all these matters that will, choice, decision, affection come into play as well as the intellect. There are no pure intellects; there never have been and there never will be. 'Faith', said William Law, 'is the power by which we give ourselves up to anything.' [11] Our intellects can prevent us from giving ourselves up to the wrong things and can prevent us from giving ourselves up in the wrong way; but we cannot live, nor even believe in anything or anybody, with the intellect alone. It is with our intellects rather that we are enabled *to doubt*, and that is a high and human prerogative, though Christians seldom have the courage to say so. Professor Susan Stebbing shrewdly remarked that the 'prevalence of doubt—for all belief is founded on preliminary doubt—is the supreme characteristic of man, that which makes him distinctively *human* and enlightened, whereas "the ignorant doubts little, the drunkard still less, and the madman never".'[12] And George Macdonald boldly claimed that 'a man may be haunted with doubts and only grow thereby in faith. . . . Doubt must precede every deeper assurance; for uncertainties are what we first see when we look into a region hitherto unknown, unexplored, unannexed'.[13] I would add that if in this or any other time there is to be a renewal of Christian belief, of faith in a Living God, it will be in part the outcome of searching and rigorous doubting, not least on the part of those who fancy that they are already the faithful. Some minds at any rate will come to a virile faith only when they have looked fearlessly into all the possibilities of doubt. And I do not think that the following words of a Russian theologian are extravagant or lacking in integrity, though at first sight they may shock us; 'The existence of God (he says) is known by an act of madness, daring and love; it is to throw the thread of life into the heavens in the certainty that it will take hold there without any guarantee of causality; it is a dumb, beseeching act; it is a prayer'.[14]

This brings me to my last introductory point, at which, for reasons that you will perceive, I can do little more than hint. I have been asked to speak to you about Christian belief; but that, after all, is an ambiguous expression. It may mean what present-day Christians believe; but I am not particularly anxious to interest you in what present-day Christians believe, nor for that matter in what Christians of other days believed. I am anxious that you should be interested in God—not in what men believe about God, but in what (if anything) he has to say for himself. And I suspect that what he has to say for himself will make what we believe about him seem pretty pale and arid. What I mean is that I am not concerned to justify our present-day Christianity. I cannot say, of course, that I am concerned to justify God, for that would be blasphemous. What I hope is that we are all concerned to discover whether there is a God who can speak for himself, even if what he says reveals the bankruptcy and futility of present-day Christianity. The at one time well-known words of Matthew Arnold are not out of date: 'At the present moment (he said) two things about the Christian religion must surely be clear to anybody with eyes in his head. One is, that men cannot do without it; the other, that they cannot do with it as it is.'[15] Or again, I have felt that the following words, which I first read about ten years ago, are dreadfully apposite to our condition: 'Religions, as we all know, can go on existing after they have ceased to function. The doctrine is still taught and—so it seems— accepted; the rites, the customs, the ceremonies, the paraphernalia remain. There seems hardly any change at all, but the old words and terms sound hollow; dullness creeps in and takes the lustre away from things that once stirred and invigorated the hearts of men.'[16] It matters little whether what we Christians call 'our religion' can again stir and invigorate the hearts of men; but it is worth inquiring whether there is a living God, a Lord Christ, a Holy Spirit, who can still speak to men and stir and invigorate them.

My business, I take it, is to assist you in making that inquiry for yourselves. In other words, our place to-day is in the mine and not in the mint of Christian doctrine.

I have already encroached upon my proper subject for to-day which is 'belief in God', and said perhaps more than I ought to have said at this stage. Now I must start afresh. The complaint is often made, and often justly made, that theologians in the books they write, and clergymen when they speak in places where men are prepared to listen to them, take too much for granted, do not start far enough back, and use words and expressions, without defining or explaining them, that are strange and foreign to the vocabulary of this age. The result is that the ordinary reader or hearer cannot tell whether they are talking sense or nonsense. I expect that I shall have occasion in the course of these lectures to offer you some definitions, but I cannot define *God*, at any rate not the God in whom Christians believe. God is, if I may put it so, by definition indefinable. He is infinite, but that is not to say that he is indefinite. Many quite definite things can be said about him, but he cannot be compressed within the terms of any definition. To insist that God shall be defined in terms that we can comprehend is to be like the children of Israel who refused to be satisfied with the Eternal, Invisible God that Moses and the Prophets proclaimed to them, and who insisted on erecting idols of wood or stone which they could see with their eyes and touch with their hands. Any definition of God that purported to be at all adequate would be an idol of the mind.

Is, then, any and every attempt to conceive God in our minds, and to describe him in words, inevitably idolatrous and mistaken? If there be a God, is the most that we can do to bow the head and to remain silent? Obviously everything I have to say depends on the answer to that question; therefore we must consider it carefully.

When James Knowles told Mr. Gladstone that Tennyson had said to him: 'The vast majority of Englishmen picture to themselves God as an illimitable clergyman with a long beard', Mr. Gladstone is reported to have made the surprising reply: 'That is the best argument in favour of the Established Church which I have ever heard.' [17] That is not a reply which it would occur to anyone to make in these days, but I fancy Mr. Gladstone was making the point that it is better to think of God even as an illimitable clergyman than not to think of him at all.

I am deliberately treating the question, What is God like? before the question, Does God exist? It might be possible to prove the existence of a god, in whose existence nobody could take the faintest interest. Some people have laboured hard to prove the existence of a First Cause with capital letters; it is not for me to say that they have laboured in vain. I must, however, confess that I have never myself been able to work up any interest in a First Cause. Let us not be like the American statesman who once sent out notices to his friends to say that he was going to be married, but without mentioning to whom. Let us first decide what kind of a God we are talking about; then and only then shall we know if it is worth while to inquire whether he exists. Only then, too, can we know what sort of evidences there might be that he does exist.

That is why I must at this point deal with the question of what is called 'anthropomorphism'. Anthropomorphism means the use of terms that are applicable to men in speaking of God or of anything other than what is human. I am accustomed to say that my dog is both wise and, when he accompanies me to chapel, devout; and that is to speak anthropomorphically. In an even broader sense, the word 'anthropomorphism' calls attention to the fact, which some people are strangely inclined to overlook, that human beings can think only in a human way and speak only in human language. 'Man never knows how anthropomorphic he is', says Dr. Tennant, 'especially perhaps when he is an intellectualistic misanthropomorphist.' [18] If we are going to think and speak about God at all, we have no other than human terms in which to do so. To think of God as the Life-force or as cosmic energy, or as the Absolute or as the Eternal Values or as the Moral Law, is not to rise above anthropomorphism, but to describe God in a human though non-personal manner.

Herbert Spencer tried to overcome this difficulty by substituting for God 'the Unknowable' (again with a capital letter), but this did not prevent him from describing his *ersatz*-deity in human terms, for, as has been wittily observed, in the course of Spencer's philosophy we are afforded far more information about the Unknowable than the combined efforts of revelation and theology have yet given us concerning God.[19]

The question here to which we really want to know the answer is whether we are justified in thinking of God in terms that are applicable to human personality—whether, to put it as simply as possible, God is like a thing or like a person. Will our relationship with things or our relationship with other persons help us the better to understand what God is like? The question is not whether we can rightly think of God as being just like a human person, but whether what we know as personality carries us nearer to the truth about God than any alternative conceptions that are within our reach. Observe that even if we described God as 'impersonal' we should still be using a human term; no others are available to us. Whatever terms we apply to God will be analogous or analogical, that is to say, we shall be using them not because they are completely adequate for their purpose, but because they point to some genuine, though incomplete, resemblance between God and what is either personal or impersonal. Eric Gill, who certainly believed that God is personal, said: 'Every description of God must be inadequate; there can be no proper description of the indescribable in words derived from the description of material things. No description of God can be more than analogical.' [20]

By all means, recognize the limitations of human language, and its insufficiency even to express what we can intuitively perceive, not only in God, but in one another and in the beauty of nature and art.

> The flowering moments of the mind
> Drop half their petals in our speech.

But also recognize that if we are to go on speaking at all, we must do the best we can with the language and the images that are available to us.

What we want to know is not whether to think of God as personal will enable us to elaborate a satisfactory speculative theory about the nature of deity, but whether God is personal in this sense that he can communicate with us and we can respond to him. Is there a God with whom personal intercourse is possible? Is there a God who makes personal demands upon us, who can influence and succour us, as a man influences and succours his friend or as a father his child?

Now, the traditional arguments for the existence of God, which, by the way, you will not find in the Bible or in the creeds of the Church, scarcely touch this vital question. I mean, for example, the argument that the existence of contingent or finite being implies the existence of necessary or infinite being, or the argument that the idea of causation implies the existence of a first cause, or the argument that the characteristics of the world point to an over-all purpose or design and therefore to a designer. The last of these arguments, known as the teleological argument, is indeed more important than the others. It can no longer be sustained in the traditional form that was associated with the name of the pre-Darwinian Archdeacon Paley, a name familiar to many generations of Cambridge undergraduates in connexion with little-go. But the argument from design ought not to be written off. It has been massively restated in the light of the scientific view of the universe by Dr. Tennant in his *Philosophical Theology*, and you will find a summary of Tennant's argument in a book by J. S. Bezzant, entitled *Aspects of Belief*.[21]

But if there is a personal God, it is in our personal experience that we shall expect to find the strongest evidences of his existence.

The sort of question a man has to ask here is whether his sense of obligation to tell the truth and to seek the truth, irrespective of his own interests or of the interests or dictates of society, is self-explanatory or not. He has to ask whether the sense of an absolute moral demand pressing upon him, from above as it were, is accounted for if there is indeed on the throne of the universe a Lord God who is entitled to press such a demand on him—and whether it is not altogether unaccountable in the end, if there isn't. Or again there is the sense of obligation to respect other persons, even when they seem very unrespectable, the sense a man has that he ought not to manipulate other persons as he may manipulate things. This sense of obligation is explained if over the human world there is an Eternal Father who endows his children with freedom and responsibility in order that they may learn what it is to be members of a universal family and may find fulfilment in a universal communion of persons.

You must distinguish the sense of personal, moral obligation from all the impersonal, natural constraints to which you are also subject. A hot day constrains you to open the window or to wear light clothes; the telephone rings, alas! and you are constrained to lift the receiver. But should a voice at the other end of the telephone ask you to do something that involves deceiving a friend or soiling your own integrity, even if the proposed act is to your own interest and can be represented as for the benefit of society, you are aware of quite a different kind of constraint. There is a demand upon your conscience, to which you by no means automatically respond, to which in fact you may fail to respond, but which is inescapably there, and which, if you fail to respond to it, leaves you with a conviction of guilt.

What is the source of this strange demand, of this moral constraint, which is so like the demand that a good man may make upon us, and yet is still there even if there is no good man to voice it? It is possible to lose sight of this great question in a tangle of psychological and epistemological sophistication, but when all is said and done the question comes back upon us and requires to be answered. We do not, of course, feel the full force of the moral imperative when we are sitting listening to a lecture or arguing in our rooms with our feet on the mantelpiece. We experience its full force when we are fiercely tempted to refuse its demands, when our passions or our interests or the pressures of society and even sometimes our best friends are urging us to do something which the voice of conscience plainly tells us we ought not to do. This experience, which is both a universal experience and an intimate individual experience, stands up and makes sense if there is a holy God, a personal God, in whom we live and move and have our being. Does it in the last resort stand up and make sense otherwise?

This consideration can be put in a more general and abstract way. Beauty, truth, goodness, love—these are meaningful only for persons, for conscious, rational, responsible beings. If you believe that these values are not merely transitory, accidental illusions of the human mind—'epiphenomena' is the technical term— but are part of the nature of things, and have their ground in the structure of ultimate reality, does it not follow that there is an eternal personal Being for whom and in whom these values exist, independently of human persons who are always passing away? Aesthetic and moral values, so far as we can tell, cannot exist apart from a mind that experiences them. If there is a God, they stand up, and the value we assign to them has an explanation and a sanction. Moreover, in this case, artists and scientists as well as moralists are not merely expressing themselves or serving the State or following an unaccountable hunch, but have the high vocation to think God's thoughts after him. Thus it is a fair question whether in the final analysis the arts and the sciences can be justified if there is no personal God who confers absolute worth upon them, although obviously it is possible for people to cultivate them without realizing this, since many people do so.

You may have come across the suggestion that a personal God is merely a psychological projection, the result of a 'father-complex', or a product of wishful thinking. This suggestion was more often made twenty years ago, when those terms enjoyed the freshness of a new invention, than it is now. All the same, it needs to be looked at still. Christians have no interest in denying that the idea of God may be in the psychological sense a projection. If God exists and is in any measure knowable, obviously the idea of God must arise and develop somehow in the human mind, and psychology may usefully uncover the processes by which it does so. A child's relation to his father may play an important part in enabling him to conceive of God. The projection theory in itself is perfectly compatible with the existence of a personal God. The idea of 'the world' or of 'the uniformity of nature' is also in this sense a projection; one can recognize that, and still reasonably hold that the world exists and that the uniformity of nature is not a pure phantasy of the human mind to which nothing in reality corresponds. The significant question here is not whether the idea of God or of anything else is a projection, but whether it is no more than a projection; and that must be decided on other grounds than that of the psychological investigation of processes that occur in the human mind.

Likewise the suggestion that the idea of a personal God is a product of wishful thinking is quite as consistent with the belief that there is a personal God as with the belief that there isn't. If men wish to believe in God, why do they wish to do so? Their wishes may certainly deceive them, and I should allow that there has been plenty of deceptive, wishful thinking mixed up with religion as with politics and a hundred other things. But men's wishes may also lead them to what is there. The wish to believe in God may be like a plant stretching out its tendrils to water. If that happens, it is because water exists; it is not evidence that the existence of water is an illusion. Admittedly, things do not exist because we desire them; but from the fact that we desire them it does not follow that they do not exist. A man sleepless with pain may long passionately for the dawn or for relief; it does not follow that the dawn will not arrive or that relief will not come to him. It is, indeed, a very superficial view that can dismiss the God in whom Christians believe as merely a product of wishful thinking. It is by no means clear that men do really wish to believe in a God like this. It is, to say the least, equally reasonable to hold that unbelief in this God is due to the fact that men don't wish to believe in him. For he is not only a God who consoles and t rengthens, but a God who makes awful and most uncomfortable demands which require, if need be, the surrender of life itself. In other words, wishful thinking can work both ways, and an appeal to it as a criterion of the existence or non-existence of a personal God merely confuses the issue or leaves it where it was before.[22]

It is one of the curiosities of agnosticism that it supposes that there is something unworthy in thinking of God as personal, and that it is more devout to think of him as entirely beyond the reach of the human mind. But the idea that the divine being is so sublime, so great, so ineffable as to be incapable of personal intercourse with men is, when you think it out, to limit and confine the power of God; it is to say that God cannot reveal himself, that he cannot get through to human beings. Certainly we should be on our guard against unworthy ideas of God, against making him in our own image; but we should also be on our guard against turning him into something inferior to our own image, and that is the mistake that is made by those who insist that deity or the Absolute must be impersonal or unknowable. He is unfathomable no doubt, but that is quite a different thing from saying he is unknowable.

And in future lectures, we shall be inquiring whether a great deal more may not be known about God than we have considered so far.

NOTES

[1] *Christianity and the Religions of the World*, p. 79.
[2] *The Tablet*, 26th July 1947, p. 55.
[3] Tillich, *The Shaking of the Foundations*, p. 79.
[4] Tillich, op cit., pp. 79f.
[5] Laberthonnière, *Critique du Laicisme*, p. 205.
[6] F. C. Bryan, *Concerning the Way*, p. 47.
[7] John Oman, *The Natural and the Supernatural*, p. 147.
[8] *Journal*, pp. 169f.
[9] *Theism and Humanism*, p. 268.
[10] *Grammar of Assent*, p. 344.
[11] Quoted in *Papers read before the Synthetic Society*, 1896-1908, p. 208.
[12] *Pragmatism and French Voluntarism*, p. 259.
[13] C. S. Lewis, *George Macdonald*, p. 70.
[14] E. Lampert, *The Divine Realm*, p. 43.
[15] *God and the Bible*, p. 372.
[16] Erich Meissner, *Germany in Peril*, p. 37.
[17] See Arthur Ponsonby, *Henry Ponsonby*, p. 26.
[18] *Philosophical Theology*, i. 198.
[19] F. C. S. Schiller, *Riddles of the Sphinx*, p. 20.
[20] *The Necessity of Belief*, p. 269. Cp. P. T. Forsyth, *The Work of Christ*, p. 210: 'It is not easy to find a word that has no defect, since all words, even the greatest, are made from the dust and spring from our sandy passions, earthly needs, and fleeting thoughts; and they are hard to stretch to the measure of eternal things without breaking under us somewhere.'
[21] Chapter iii, pp. 70-110.
[22] Cp. H. H. Farmer, *God and Men*, pp. 31f.; H. R. Mackintosh, *The Christian Apprenhension of God*, p. 20; W. R. Matthews, *God in Christian Thought and Experience*, pp. 22f.

II

GOD AND MANKIND

*

IN my first lecture I spoke about the context of unfathomed mystery in which Christian belief ought to be considered, and apart from which it must appear to be either meaningless or otiose. Then I tried to fasten your attention on the great question whether we can rightly think and speak of God as *personal*. I did that, not only because this is in itself a question of cardinal importance, but because unless God is both knowable and personal, in the sense that personal communication with him is possible, we can hardly have any personal interest in his existence, nor will anything else that Christians believe seem credible.

But a man does well to have scruples about describing God as personal. It is anyhow, misleading to describe him as *a person*, though highly orthodox divines sometimes do so. It is well to have scruples here, because it is extremely easy to slip into the position where we make God in our own image, and suppose that personality in God is limited and imperfect as it is in man, even in a good man. Now a man, or the best of men, can have only a limited number of friends, and a limited though larger circle of acquaintances. None of us can be equally interested in everybody, not even in everybody we meet. None of us can be on terms of personal relationship, on speaking terms or, what is more to the point, on caring terms, with all the persons whom we pass in the street, or with whom we come into contact, for instance with every clerk in every booking office from which we casually buy a railway ticket.

When God is described as personal, we are liable to suppose that he, too, can be really interested in only a limited number of human beings—a very much larger number than ourselves no doubt, but still only in a selection from the whole human race. And, at first sight, we may get the impression that we are encouraged, indeed expected, to suppose this to be so both from what the Bible says about God and from the accepted beliefs of

Christians. For doesn't the Bible say—in the Old Testament, that God chose only one nation, the Jews, presumably because he was peculiarly interested in them or specially cared for them—and in the New Testament, that he singled out the Christians, those who believed in Christ and were baptized, and treated them as an elect or select section of the race? And don't Christians hold, though they may not put it quite so bluntly, that God really cares only for religious people or for good people or for orthodox believers? Don't Christians, anyhow, give the impression that they and their God are interested in the man in the street only in so far as he may become a man in the pew? Don't Christians look upon pagans or neo-pagans as aliens to themselves and therefore as aliens to God, and on 'secular' affairs as though they were much inferior to religious affairs and on God as interested mainly in the latter? There is no doubt that this impression exists. I have frequently received it myself, and for all I know may have given grounds for it. But I am also sure that this leads to a gross misrepresentation of God—of the God of the Bible, of the God and Father of our Lord Jesus Christ.

I want therefore to-day to inquire into the way in which God is in a living relation to *mankind*, to all the members of our race, and indeed to the whole cosmos.

Let us begin with the cosmos. According to the Bible and the creeds, God is the creator of heaven and earth, of all things visible and invisible. This means that the universe in its entirety is not self-existent or self-explanatory, but is dependent on the creative action of the Eternal God. The Bible and traditional Christian belief, we all know, conceived the universe to be constructed on a very much smaller scale than we have to try to conceive it now. Indeed, the contrast between the size of the universe, its extension in space and its duration in time, as the ancients thought of it and as we think of it, is staggering to the imagination. In the mind of anyone who reflects upon this contrast the question inevitably arises whether it is still possible to believe that God, a personal God, is the creator of such a universe as scientific investigation has disclosed, and also whether it is still possible to believe that in so vast a universe man is as important as used to be supposed.

Let it be granted at once that it is prodigiously difficult to *imagine* how a personal God—for that is what we are talking about, and not some recondite form of cosmic energy—can be in a living relation to the whole universe. The attempt to imagine any such relation quickly dizzies the mind. But even in the old days no one in his senses supposed that it was possible for a finite mind to *imagine* what it felt like to be God the creator of all things visible and invisible. The dizzying extension of the size of the universe raises no new problem for the *reason* as distinguished from the imagination. It must mean, indeed, that the power of God is even greater and more astonishing than men of old had realized, but they held emphatically that his power was infinite. Thus it is fair to say that every new discovery of the range of the universe and of the complexity of the microcosm as well as of the macrocosm serves to document and fill in the outline of what had already been inferred about God from the cruder and very small-scale map that alone was open to the vision of men in biblical times.

The formidable difficulty here is that which concerns the importance of *man* in such a universe and the possibility of *man's* being in personal relations with a God of such unimaginable power. But here too the difficulty, in so far as it is a new one, is much more of the imagination than of the reason. At first, it is true, man, and indeed the earth on which we live, seem to be dwarfed into such insignificance that it seems to be the height of presumption to suppose that we or it are of any importance at all. If we took this seriously, we should fall into a panic about the worthwhileness of anything we do; and, as a matter of fact, Christians as well as other people did get pretty panicky when the homeliness of the little universe to which they had been accustomed was first threatened by the incoming tide of scientific discovery. Is it then only the congenital conceit of humanity which makes us go on thinking that we and our doings and our concerns are still important?

When we ask a question like that—and we have reason enough to ask it, for God knows we are prone enough to conceit—we are overlooking a consideration which tells in almost the opposite direction. For however vast the universe is, man alone among created beings, so far as we can tell, knows anything about its vastness. The universe itself is unconscious, dumb, inarticulate, irresponsible. In man alone the universe becomes conscious of itself, and acquires articulation, meaning, and the possibility of conscious glory. Thus, what at first sight diminishes man's stature, on a profounder view heightens it. To put it in another way: over against the vastness of the universe, man's status as an *object*, as a thing, as a measurable entity, dwindles away to nothingness; but at the same time his status as a *subject*, as a person, is heightened, for it is man who measures the cosmos and inquires into its laws, and finds its immensity bewildering. The universe cannot measure itself, or inquire into its own laws, or realize in the smallest degree how bewildering it is.[1] Only a person, only a being endowed with reason and imagination, can do that.

Then again, does this immense extension of space and time make any substantial difference to those elements in our experience which are nonetheless real for being unmeasurable and intangible? Does mere size have any bearing on those things which are most characteristic of personality and personal relationships—the capacity for thought and speech, for making moral and aesthetic judgments, for recognizing moral obligation, for friendship and love? Unless we are prepared to cut the ground from under our own feet, including the ground on which we have discovered the vastness of the universe—unless we are prepared to say that only what we experience as quantity is real and that what we experience as quality is an illusion—unless we are prepared to wash meaning and value right out of the universe—then we have to confess that its size makes no decisive difference to the possibility of there being a personal God who takes a personal interest in us and whose purpose for the universe of his creation becomes evident only where there are persons who can responsibly enter in to it. Thus it may be agreed that the late Dr. Streeter spoke a word that is both true and apt when he said that 'a man's passion for his ladylove takes up no more room in space than his affection for his great-aunt; the difference is one of intensity and quality, not of size. The kind of disapprobation with which a fashionable undergraduate regards a man who wears the wrong tie and that with which Elijah viewed the prophets of Baal, is a difference that may be called "world-wide"; but that does not mean that it is one to which the diameter of the earth is in the smallest degree relevant.'[2]

We may conclude in fact that, so far as size goes, the way in which we construe the physical universe and the way in which the Bible construes it, our large-scale view and the Bible's small-scale view, may be like two alphabets in which the same thing may be differently said and be equally true. That is to say, the relation of the universe to a personal God and our relation to it and to him are not necessarily different from what they were, because they now look different. Or, put it like this, a sentence is neither more nor less true if it is written in larger or smaller letters. So the Bible's affirmation that 'the heavens declare the glory of God and the firmament showeth his handiwork' may still be true when we see that there is a great deal of it and a great deal more to it than our forefathers realized. Perhaps I have spent too long on the matter of the size of the universe; that may be because I must confess that it oppresses my own imagination, even when my reason tells me that it ought not to do so. All I will add is this, that the vastness of the universe should induce in us a wholesome sense of humility, and moderate our tendency to cocksureness. But even here we did not need to wait for modern discoveries to teach that lesson. At any time a little solitary reflection high up in the Alps or in the Lake District would do as well.

We ought indeed now to turn our attention to the earth upon which we live. Its story, the manner in which it came into existence, and its evolution, are also very different from what the Bible and traditional Christian belief supposed. Can we still believe that it is the creation of a personal God? Is man more than an incidental product of its evolution and a part of the animal world? Modern theologians are wont to say that the assertion at the beginning of the Book of Genesis that God created the earth and all that dwells upon it, and man as the crown of his work, is unaffected by scientific discoveries. All that these discoveries have done is to show that the act of divine creation was much more protracted and intricate than was previously realized. The real gist, it is said, of the Genesis story is that *God* is the creator and that what he made was originally good, so that any idea that matter is inherently evil is excluded. But there is more that needs to be said.

The first chapter of Genesis conveys the notion that God's work in creation was a finished work. However long it actually took, the creation was complete once man was launched upon the scene, and then God rested. But the Bible as a whole, in which references to the early chapters of Genesis are few and far between, corrects this facile notion. God's work as creator is a continuous work. It is to be conceived dynamically, not statically. 'My Father is working still, and I am working', Christ is represented as saying. [3]

We can now see, though not all Christians do yet see, that the stories at the beginning of Genesis should be regarded not as history nor as pre-history, but as mythology. They are not to be understood as descriptions of what occurred in the year 4004 B.C., nor to be re-interpreted as referring to what occurred thousands or millions of years before that date. They constitute a mythology in which the *permanent* relation of God to the world, and to mankind in particular, is pictorially and profoundly depicted. Not once upon a time did God create, but at every moment of time he is creating. He is responsible for the whole process, and not merely for having given it an initial impetus.

Man is endowed with intelligence so that he can discover the manner of God's incessant creative activity, the laws of his working—the laws of nature as we call them. Kilvert in his diary quotes Bishop Alexander of Derry as saying that 'natural laws are not chains about the living God, but threads which he holds in his hands',[4] and that was well said. Happily for us God works in an orderly, even in a mechanical, manner. Otherwise we should not be able to trace the laws of his working. The natural world provides an indispensable framework or underground for human or personal life. As Professor Farmer has said: 'That there is . . . a rigidly mechanical aspect of events is obvious; it is obvious, too, that this is very fortunate for persons such as we are, for otherwise we could never live a personal life in our world at all; it is only because the fire can be relied on to boil the kettle, and sound-waves to carry our speech, that we can indulge in that highly personal activity called a tea-party. One of our prime tasks is to get to know what these mechanisms of our world are and to use them; and natural science . . . is just the organised and systematic attempt to get to know what they are.' [5]

What then about the peculiar characteristics of man and the peculiar relation in which he stands to God? Man is certainly part of nature. He arises out of nature; but also he stands in a personal relation to God, a *responsibly* personal relation, and that cannot be said of the rest of the creation. Genesis makes the pregnant statement that God made man in his own image—so pregnant a statement that huge tomes have been written and are still being written about its meaning. No doubt it implies more than whoever first penned the words realized, though it may be doubted whether it implies as much as many theologians have extracted from it.

Remember that the story of the creation of man ('Adam' means 'man') and also of his fall is to be understood not as the history of a first man or of a first human couple (about which we have no information whatever), but as a mythology which illuminates the relation in which *mankind*, every man, always stands to God. That man is made in the image of God means that God is able personally to communicate with man, to speak to him and to be answered by him. It means also that God endows man with a share in his own freedom, and calls him to co-operate in the work of creation, in the unfolding of all the possibilities of manifesting the divine glory that are latent in God's creative purpose. Man is free to respond to God and to co-operate with God, but he can also refuse. This is the prerogative, at once magnificent and awful, of the human race.

Similarly, the myth of the fall of man does not point to a single event in history or pre-history, which is the cause of all the troubles of our race, but it points to a contradiction that there is in the being of every man. Every man is made in the image of God so that he can willingly live in harmony with nature, with his fellow men and with God. But as we all know when we contemplate human history and human society or when we each look within ourselves, man's existence is very far from being harmonious. 'Society is like a collection of hedgehogs driven together for the sake of warmth', said the cynical Schopenhauer, but the aphorism is not merely cynical. And the distracted state of the individual man was put quaintly, but with characteristic faithfulness, by Thomas Fuller: 'Pride', he said, 'calls me to the window, gluttony

c

to the table, wantonness to the bed, laziness to the chimney, ambition commands me to go upstairs, and covetousness to come down. Vices, I see, are as well contrary to themselves as to virtue.' [6]

The law of man's nature 'is love, a harmonious relation of life to life in obedience to the divine centre and source of his life. This law is violated when man seeks to make himself the centre and source of his own life'.[7] The fall of man means that both collectively and individually he does violate the law of his being. He does not keep in his place. He is not content to abide in loving obedience to God. He is always and restlessly seeking to make himself the centre of existence. Egotism or egocentricity is the most comprehensive, as well as the most acute, definition of the sin of man. As William Law said: 'The kingdom of *self* is the Fall of man, or the great apostasy from the Life of God in the Soul; and everyone wherever he be, that lives unto Self, is still under the Fall and great apostasy from God.' [8]

The rediscovery of the fallenness of man and what is called the dogma of 'original sin', has in our time so gone to the heads of some Christians, and of some other people too, that they talk as though this were the whole truth about man, which explains everything. But 'original sin', which anyhow is a misleading expression,[9] does not explain everything, and the doctrine of the Fall, so far from justifying a pessimistic or fatalistic view of human nature, provides a ground of hope that otherwise would be lacking. For to say that man is fallen is to say that he is not at present in his proper state, the state where he belongs, the state for which he is made, the state which befits the original constitution of his being. It is then possible for him to be restored to his right state, whereas, if to be a sinner or an egoist is his original, fundamental, and proper state, there is no hope of his being rescued from it.

Bishop Westcott put it thus: 'No view of the human state is so inexpressibly sad as that which leaves out the Fall. The existence of evil in its many forms, as self-will and suffering and vice and crime, cannot be gainsaid; and, if this evil belongs to the essence of man as created, then there can be no prospect of relief here or hereafter.' [10] The point was made more piquantly by G. K. Chesterton when he said, 'If I wish to dissuade a man from drink-

ing his tenth whisky and soda, I slap him on the back and say, "Be
a man !" No one who wished to dissuade a crocodile from eating
its tenth explorer would slap it on the back and say, "Be a
crocodile !" ' [11]

The original truth about man, about every man, is that he is in
the image of God. He is held in a personal relationship of responsibility to God, whether or not he knows or acknowledges it.
While he may try to live independently of God and to be the
centre of his own existence, God never lets him go. God does not
let him get away with the monstrous illusion that he is or can
make himself the centre of everything. Hence the contradiction
that there is in man. Hence both the grandeur and the misery of
man. Hence, on the one hand, his splendid achievements and the
relics and sparkles of glory which encompass him even at his
worst—this springs from his personal relation to the God of all
glory. But hence, on the other hand, his profound discontent, the
discords and diseases with which he is always labouring and to
which he constantly succumbs—this springs from his vain deter-
mination to live for himself and unto himself.

I do not know that the paradox of the grandeur and the misery
of man has been more eloquently or movingly expressed by a
modern theologian than in the two following paragraphs from a
little known book that is very hard to come by. First, the grandeur; then the misery.

'We inherit greatness and breathe it. Earth and sky and day and
night; stars in the naked heavens, breathings of wind, and the
coming of spring; hill and plain, rolling tracts, and river and sea;
the mist on the long, wet moor, and above it the black, baleful
cloud; fleets and camps, cities and realms; valour and power,
science, trade, Churches, causes, arts, charities; the fidelities of
peace and the heroisms of war, the rhythm of order and the stream
of progress; the generations that go under and the civilizations
that survive; the energies unseen, the vanished past, the forgotten
and the unforgettable brave; the majesty of the moral hero and
the splendour of the public saint; agonies, love, and man's uncon-
querable mind—Oh, we have a great world, great glories, great
records, great prospects, and great allies ! We inherit greatness,
and we inhabit promise. . . .

'But as our sun rises there is a rising cloud. In the moving soul there is a frail seam, an old wound, a tender sore. The stout human heart has a wearing ache and a haunting fear. There is a hollow in the soul's centre, in its last hold no fortress, and in its sanctuary no abiding God. A vanity blights the glory of time, a lameness falls on the strenuous wing, our sinew shrinks at certain touches, and we halt on our thigh; pride falters, and the high seems low, and the hour is short, and the brief candle is out, and what is man that he is accounted of? There is a day of the Lord upon all that is haughty, on lofty tower, and tall cedar, and upon all pleasant imagery. And misery, sin and death grow great as all our triumph dwindles on the sight. . . . The greatness of the soul is more apparent in the greatness of its misery than in the triumph of its powers.' [12]

For a man, for a race, to be in that condition is to be under a curse. In the 'untragic atmosphere of intellectual West-Ends' that may seem too strong, too bad, a word. But where it is experienced as a matter of life and death no milder word suffices to sum up the human situation. To perceive that is to perceive why, according to Christian belief, mankind stands in need, and has always stood in need, of a universal deliverance and of a universal deliverer. Whether there has been such a deliverance or redemption, whether there is such a deliverer or redeemer, we have yet to consider. But it is never easy to see how a need may be met, unless one has felt the force of the need. 'They that are whole have no need of a physician, but they that are sick.' Christian faith is faith in a God who has to deal with a race that is sick, as well as with individuals who are sick. It is faith in a God who is able to deal with this universal disease, and who is doing so in the course of history. The Bible, which the creeds summarize, is the witness to God's method of healing mankind, his method of bringing many sons unto glory notwithstanding their shame.

I do not mean that the Bible or Christian belief supplies a complete or detailed explanation of what God is doing with mankind or with each individual man in history. Very much is hidden, not only of the future but also of the past and of the present. The claim of the Bible is not to make known everything that we should like to know about the ways of God with men, but to tell us sufficient of what we need to know for practical purposes.[13] In this sense Christian belief is not speculative but pragmatic, although Christians have indulged in plenty of fruitless speculation in their time. 'Our Lord came among us,' said Dean Church, 'not to clear up the perplexity but to show us which side to take,' [14] and that can be said of the whole Biblical revelation.

This is the first time I have used the word 'revelation', which is often on the lips of theologians, so I will pause to indicate its meaning, or at least the sense in which I use the word. I wish to disown two things that revelation has been taken to mean, and still is in some circles. First, revelation has been taken to mean that God has communicated to the faithful certain statements of truth in the form of propositions, the infallibility of which is guaranteed. The view may be taken that the whole Bible is thus guaranteed to be exempt from error, or it may be the creeds, or the pronouncements of the pope. It is a corollary of this view that Christian belief can be deduced from a set of revealed propositions. There are many objections to this way of regarding revelation, into which I will not enter as I want to be positive rather than negative, and anyhow its mistaken character is increasingly being confessed, even among Roman Catholics. I would only point out that it arises from, or leads to, the assumption that human language is an adequate medium for the expression of the truth about God and mankind, at least to the extent that logical deductions can reliably be made from it without recourse to empirical evidence.[15] But as Streeter said: 'the grandest of all follies is to imagine that any words we use or any definitions we can frame about God and his dealings with man, can have that kind of equivalence to the reality which alone could make them premises for valid logical deduction.' [16]

The other false way of regarding revelation is that which simply equates it with discovery. It is true that, when we discover something which we had not realized before, we sometimes say, 'it came to me as a revelation', and it is significant that we do say that, for it may be that God has then unveiled to us some fact to which hitherto our passions or our obtuseness had blinded us. But the question here is whether in our personal experience the only operative factor is man who discovers, who seeks and finds, or whether God is not also personally active in removing the veils which obscure man's vision. Just as if by the word 'good' all you meant was pleasurable or socially useful, it would be better to eliminate the word 'good' from your vocabulary, so if by the word 'revelation' all you meant was man's power of discovering things, it would be better to eliminate the word 'revelation' from your theology, since its use would only rot the question and confuse the issue.

There can be no doubt that according to the Bible and Christian belief, God is so personally related to men that he can, and does, make himself known to them and opens their eyes to what they would not see if he were not also seeking them and finding them. God reveals himself personally—that is, as a man makes himself known to his friend and not as a dictator imposes the correct party-line on his subjects. God reveals himself as one person affects or influences another without infringing his personal independence.

Professor Dorothy Emmet has said that the term 'revelation' should be used 'to mean something which we do not invent or construct, but something which impinges on us and which our minds have to seek to interpret.' [17] The question then is, where does God impinge on mankind? As we have seen, the whole universe may speak to man of God. 'The heavens declare the glory of God, and the firmament showeth his handiwork.' But they do not do so explicitly or articulately. In fact, to some minds they have spoken not of God, but of a devil; and the natural world in itself, with its silence, its ruthlessness, and its mystery, is at least ambiguous in its testimony. It is because God, the personal God, has impinged on men at particular moments and in special ways and has raised up interpreters of his revealing activity that men have been led to confess that he impinges on them everywhere, in hidden as well as in open ways, through his silences as well as through his speech.

Thus the core of the Biblical revelation of God is to be found in his dealings with a chosen people, with prophets and apostles who interpret his ways, and with the Man Christ Jesus in whom all culminates. But the Bible does not restrict or confine God's self-revealing to the chosen people or to individuals who are singled

out for particular communications of his will. The Bible may
appear to do this at times; indeed, it certainly does so in its early
stages (by which I do not mean of course the opening chapters of
Genesis). But in the end, and at its highest levels of insight, it
witnesses that all mankind is within the scope and range of God's
making himself known.

The Hebrew prophets represent the highest level of insight in
the Old Testament, and it is they who universalized the conception not only of God's rule over the world, but also of his purpose
for and dealings with mankind. Cyrus, for example, who does
not know God by his true name, is nevertheless called to be his
servant and can do his will. The mythology at the beginning of
Genesis, at any rate in its present form, dates from after the time
of the great prophets. Its symbolical account of God as the creator
of mankind and, in the myth of the universal deluge, as the judge
and redeemer of mankind,[18] reflects the prophetic insight that
what God had done and had promised to do with his people,
Israel, was the clue to what he had done and had promised to do
with the whole race and with all nations.

The men of Israel were specially enabled to see how God impinged upon them as their judge and deliverer, not only in their
private, personal experience, but also in their public, political
experience. In the prophet Hosea, we can observe how his personal experience of the infidelity of his wife enabled him to interpret the sins of his people, Israel, in terms of their infidelity to God.
Now this special revelation of God to Israel could be regarded as
an exclusive privilege of theirs, as though they were God's
favourites and he did not care about the rest of mankind. And
there was a persistent tendency so to regard the divine election of
Israel, a tendency which has persisted also in the church of Christ.
But the prophetic and the final word of the Bible about this is
that election is election not to exclusive privilege but to universal
service and universal witness. The privilege of Israel was to witness to all nations and to all men that God was personally related
to *them*, and purposed to redeem *them* as well as Israel from the
human predicament.

God's revelation of himself to Israel came not, so to speak, in
an even, continuous stream, but at critical moments or turning-

points in their national history. At the time of the Exodus when the nation, in whatever rudimentary form it then existed, was marvellously brought out of bondage in Egypt, God made himself known as the deliverer of his people. When they established themselves in Palestine and acquired a settled government, God made himself known as the righteous ruler of his people. At the time of the exile and captivity in Babylon, God made himself known as the just judge of his people, who will not tolerate idolatry or iniquity or immorality. At the time of the restoration after the exile, God made himself known as the re-creator of his people, who casts them down only that he may build them up.

Thus God has revealed himself and his relationship to mankind and to all nations, not only through his dealings with an elect people but above all at moments of crisis, change, and revolution in their history and by inspiring prophets to interpret the meaning of events that otherwise might have seemed inexplicable. This method he will follow in his supreme act of self-revelation through the Word made flesh.

It might appear to us that God should have revealed himself universally, immediately, and continuously to all mankind, but after all that is not the way in which person is revealed to person. It is at critical moments that we really get to know our friends and they get to know us—at moments of unforeseen disaster or of unforeseen success, in their reaction and ours to birth and marriage and death. Between such moments, there may be long intervals when no fresh light is struck in our personal relations and there is no sensible deepening of friendship, but then another moment of revelation comes and we are suddenly surprised.

And again, God's method in revealing himself to mankind by election and at special times corresponds with the way in which all the discoveries which he inspires are made available for the race. To us it might seem more equitable and rational that new inventions in medicine and surgery, for instance, should become known immediately to the general mind of the race and at once become available everywhere and for all. But it is not so and it could not be so, the conditions of human existence being what they are. God respects these conditions, for which indeed he is responsible, in his directly personal and self-revealing dealings with mankind. He respects the conditions of personal relationship and has refused the role of social engineer. Divine election means that God chooses particular men and particular nations for the privilege of receiving special opportunities of service to mankind and to performing tasks for the benefit of all. 'Many are called, but few are chosen.' This principle of election is woven into the texture of history, and the mystery and the blessing of it come to a head in the work of Christ.

NOTES

[1] Cp. E. Brunner, *Man in Revolt*, p. 422.
[2] B. H. Streeter, *Reality*, p. 136.
[3] John 5:17.
[4] *Kilvert's Diary*, ii. 381.
[5] H. H. Farmer, *God and Men*, pp. 38f.
[6] *Good Thoughts for Bad Times* (1863 ed.), p. 94.
[7] Reinhold Niebuhr, *The Nature and Destiny of Man*, i. 17.
[8] *Spirit of Prayer*, p. 82.
[9] Since ultimately it is not original, and is sin only in a derivative sense.
[10] B. F. Westcott, *Social Aspects of Christianity*, p. 12.
[11] Quoted by W. H. Moberly in *Foundations*, p. 284.
[12] P. T. Forsyth, *The Taste of Death and the Life of Grace*, pp. 84–7.
[13] E.g., see Deuteronomy 19:29.
[14] *Life and Letters of R. W. Church*, p. 330.
[15] The dogma of the bodily Assumption of the Virgin Mary, which has now (1950) been made compulsory.
[16] *The Buddha and the Christ*, p. 138. Cp. William Sanday in *The Pilot*, ix. 85 (January 1904): 'Every presentation of truth in human forms and in human language is of necessity relative. Even the teaching of our Lord himself could not be exempt from this condition. Much more must it attach to all subsequent attempts at the formulation of Christian doctrine. Any such formulation must always be doubly conditioned, both by the permanent limitations of the human mind, and by the temporary habits of thought of the particular age in which the formulation takes place.' See also F. C. S. Schiller, *Problems of Belief*, p. 139.
[17] *Philosophy and Faith*, p. 66.
[18] See C. H. Dodd, *The Bible To-day*, p. 114.

III

THE WORK OF CHRIST

*

MY design in these lectures is not to construct a chain of
arguments in support of Christian belief so that at the
end I might be able to say triumphantly Q.E.D. I do
not think that the truth of any belief about the nature of the
world and the meaning of human existence can be demonstrated
in that way. What I am trying to elucidate is not a chain of
arguments which would break down altogether if one link in
the chain snapped, but an interpretation of our existence and
experience in this bewildering universe—an interpretation which
is more luminous at some points than at others and which,
when all is said and done, will leave plenty of enigmas on our
hands. No interpretation, no faith, no system of belief, is demonstrable. The most that a wise man claims for the basic convictions
by which he lives is that they make more sense of all the facts with
which we have to reckon than any alternative set of convictions.

Christians are perhaps in a position to understand why this
should be so, though some of them, so far from understanding it,
hanker after watertight demonstrations—of the existence of God,
for example—and even persuade themselves that they have suc-
ceeded in fabricating them. But the God in whom they profess to
believe is a personal God who desires a personal, that is a free,
response of trust and obedience and love from the persons whom
he creates. He has therefore so constituted the world and the
minds of men that it is impossible for him to coerce them through
their intellects, as he would be able to do if his relationship to them
could be so demonstrated that every one who could take in a
logical argument was compelled to accept it. When Isaiah had his
vision of God in the temple at Jerusalem and received his commission, it is said that 'the house was filled with smoke', and this
may be taken to mean that God—being what he is and intending
us to be what we are—can reveal himself to us only by remaining
veiled.[1]

According to Christian belief all facts are related to God and speak of God, at any rate obliquely. But there are some facts which speak of him more directly than others, and moreover provide a clue which enables those who follow it to acknowledge him even where he is silent or hidden. By facts I mean things that actually exist or events that have actually happened, as distinguished from wishes or dreams or mere notions that have been conceived. Facts are also to be distinguished from mythology. A mythology may illuminate facts and help us to understand them, but is not itself necessarily a record of facts. Again, facts are to be distinguished from ideas, such as the idea of being good, which might, I suppose, be a good idea even if there were no facts to bear it out.

Christian belief appeals to facts. It makes use of mythology and it bears out certain ideas, if you like to think of it so. But the core of Christian belief is not a mythology, nor a set of timeless ideas; it is a set of facts, of facts which occurred in history and can be verified in history. This of course is also to say, again and in another way, that Christian belief cannot be demonstrated; for, as Lessing said, no historical truths can be *demonstrated*, so that nothing can be *demonstrated* by historical truths. To some minds the tie-up of Christian belief with historical facts seems either unnecessary or foolish. Gandhi, for example, wrote as follows: 'I may say I have never been interested in a historical Jesus. I should not care if it was proved by some one that the man called Jesus never lived, and that what was narrated in the Gospels was a figment of the writer's imagination. For the Sermon on the Mount would still be true for me.' [2] Or to take an example nearer home, Lowes Dickinson said: 'My difficulty about Christianity is, and always has been, that Christians make the centre of their faith the historical existence of a man at a certain age. I dare say he *did* exist, though that has been doubted. But if he *did*, what was he really like? I cannot think religion can depend upon such uncertainties.' [3]

Well, whether we like it or not, Christian belief does depend on such uncertainties, and this is a circumstance that undoubtedly raises a formidable difficulty which is not to be got over by pretending that after all historical truths can be demonstrated, or by ignoring the logical limitations from which no historical evidence can escape. I shall presently have something to say about this difficulty, but I want first to point out what the particular facts are with which Christian belief is bound up and which, Christians hold, provide the clue to the meaning of all other facts.

They are the facts of which the Bible, and especially the New Testament, contains the record. The decisive events took place in the first century of our era, though the verification of them and the further exploration of their meaning have gone on ever since. I am going to approach these decisive or original facts, in which the work of Christ can be most plainly seen, backwards. That is, I am not going to start with the year A.D. 1 or the year A.D. 30, but about the year A.D. 100 and to move back from there.

I want you then first to look at certain facts which were in the world at the end of the first century but which were not there when it began. There had sprung into existence in the cities and towns around the Mediterranean sea a new network of societies or brotherhoods, which bore the name 'Christian'. If you had been an ordinary citizen of the Roman Empire at the time, you might scarcely have noticed their existence. For, after all, there were very many religious guilds and societies in the Roman Empire (almost as many as there are in the U.S.A. today) catering for different types and classes of people, and for different nationalities. What was one more among so many?

But supposing that the existence of the Christians was brought to your notice and you came across them in Rome or Corinth or Ephesus—you might have thought at first that they were only a particular sect of the Jews and have written them off as no more than that. However, if you had looked into the matter a little further, you would have discovered that this could not be so. For, although the Jews and the Christians had originally been closely connected, they were now quite definitely separate, and indeed rival, bodies of people. But the Jews and the Christians still displayed one common and curious characteristic. Unlike the members of other religious societies, they refused to conform to the general customs, traditions and morals of the Roman world. For instance, they would not join in the worship of the Emperor, which involved no more than casting a pinch of incense before his statue, a thing that everybody else did without turning a hair or thinking anything of it. Your first impression would be that the Christians were an awkward and a peculiar lot.

But if you had been moved to go still further into the matter, and had tried to find out more about these Christian brotherhoods, you would have been struck by a number of things, of apparently contradictory things. You would have been struck by the facts that the Christians were exclusive and also inclusive, that they were powerless and also powerful, that they were authoritarian and also free.

First, like the Jews, the Christians were exclusive. They did not mix more than was necessary in society. They did not take part in the popular games and festivals. They would not even, as I have said, pay the conventional homage to the Emperor. If you were a man of the world, you would have thought their manners and their morals very strict, and odd, and perhaps rather shocking. Each Christian church was a small isolated unit, meeting almost secretly in an upstairs room in a back street. They seemed to be cut off, and to cut themselves off, from the bulk of mankind. At the same time there was much coming and going between them from one city to another and all the members felt that they belonged to a single family—that they formed a new race; that they were parts of one body; that they were the heralds and advance-guard of a common life for all men. And, indeed, the Christian brotherhoods were already strikingly inclusive. They included classes and types of people who elsewhere would not mix and were opposed to one another. Here, bound together in a closely-knit community, you found Jews and Gentiles, Greeks and barbarians, freemen and slaves, different nationalities, men and women, for women were given an equal status with men. Nothing so inclusive, so all-embracing, and at the same time so intimate as these brotherhoods, had ever been seen.

Secondly, the Christians were both powerless and powerful. Obviously, they were a quite unimportant social group; they had no influence whatever on political or economic affairs. No Christian at this time had dreamed that in a few centuries the whole Empire would have become Christian, at any rate in name, or that Caesar himself would bow before the cross. At the end of the

first century the Christians were powerless and without any prospect of power. And yet what was this power (dynamic, don't
we call it now?) that hit you in the eye? Not only did the Christians claim that they already possessed 'the powers of the age to
come' (whatever that might be); but there was no mistaking the
fact that they did possess, or were possessed by, some unearthly
power. Their morality might be austere, but it was radiant. They
were simple and uneducated folk for the most part and yet how
alive and active were their minds! Have you considered how
remarkable it is that the riff-raff of Corinth could understand
those letters of Paul's (at any rate, they thought they were worth
preserving)—the epistles to the Corinthians—which are quite
above your head, and which still puzzle our most eminent theologians? These early Christians had an astonishing intellectual
power. Moreover, they were marked by an intense vitality and
hopefulness, which were in striking contrast to the dreariness and
weariness of the world around them. The Roman Empire in A.D.
100 bore many signs of decay and death and failure of nerve, but
here in its midst, in the Christian community centres, was a new
world breaking into life.

Thirdly, the Christians were both authoritarian and free. 'Obey'
and 'obedience' were words that were frequently on their lips, and
not only on their lips. They delighted to think of themselves as
bond-servants or slaves. They were men under authority. They
knew not the watchwords of liberal democracy. They went out
of their way to acknowledge the authority of civil government
although it had already begun to persecute them. At the same
time, they spoke of liberty as glorious, and they meant it. They
were bidden to stand fast in the liberty to which they had been
called. They felt like men who had been delivered from the bondage of oppressive powers without and of unruly passions within.
They had no theory about the reconciliation of authority and
freedom—that perpetual conundrum of political and ecclesiastical
existence—but somehow they had discovered a practical solution
of the problem. *Cui servire regnare est* might well have been their
motto, 'whose service is perfect freedom'.

I am not saying that these Christian communities were perfect
or that they were exempt from stains and strains. When full allow-

ance has been made for their shortcomings, what I have said is, I believe, a fair indication of the new thing that had sprung into existence by the end of the first century. It is a fact that it had done so. What was behind it? How are we to account for it? What does it mean? Suppose now that you had taken steps to find out. Suppose you had sought out, or (to use a favourite but revolting modern word) had 'contacted', some of the leading Christians and asked them to tell you what was at the bottom of all this.

They would not all have answered in just the same way. They had no official creed, no penny catechism, no infallible pope. Their only sacred book at this time was what we know as the Old Testament, though most of the Gospels and Epistles had been written and before long would be joined with the Old Testament to make the complete Bible. But while the Christians would have told you their story in different ways—not only using different forms of thought, but also lacking detailed consistency in what they said about the work of Christ—still you would not have required unusual acumen in order to detect that their testimony was impressively congruous. The story they told you would, in fact, have been very much like what we know as the Apostles' Creed. I prefer to call it 'the apostolic testimony', for the Apostles' Creed was not drawn up till later. This is, roughly speaking, what you would have been told.

The Almighty God, the creator and ruler of the world, has suddenly and miraculously fulfilled the promises which he made to his people, Israel. For long ago, when men were wandering in the dark and refusing to follow the light that God had given them in their consciences, God had chosen one nation, Israel, through whom he intended and promised to bring back all nations to light and life and unity. But Israel had not obeyed him. Again and again, Israel had rejected God's messengers. So last of all God had sent his only-begotten Son to Israel. Jesus of Nazareth had lived as a man among them. He had been mysteriously anointed King or Messiah of Israel. He had gone about doing mighty works, and summoning the people to repent and get ready for the new age in which God's promises would be fulfilled. But him, too, they had rejected and sent to a shameful death. God had, however, raised him up and made him the head of a new people, a new race, a new humanity. Jesus, the Messiah of Israel, was now exalted to the throne of God; he was Lord of all. At the last time, the veils which at present concealed his Lordship over the world would be removed and he would be universally acknowledged as the judge and deliverer of the living and the dead.

But already, according to the apostolic testimony, the new age, of which Jesus was the herald and the king, had dawned; it had begun. It was proved by the fact that he had poured out 'Holy Spirit' on all who repented of their sins and turned to God. This Holy Spirit was a new power of love and holiness which enabled them to live a new kind of life and to live it together. This was the secret, the open secret, of those Christian brotherhoods, or communities or churches, which had been springing into existence all over the Roman Empire. God the Creator, Jesus the Messiah, and the Holy Spirit were at the bottom of these Christian communities and accounted for and explained them.

That is what they would have told you. Were they right or were they wrong? What the Christians believed was as definite as that, and not any vague ideas about the value of goodness or the desirability of a better world. If you want to make sure, you have only to read the documents, or the dossier, which we know as the New Testament.

The question, therefore, that has to be asked is whether the apostolic testimony is credible, whether it is true. It is an historical question but it is not only an historical question. It has immense implications. For if what the Christians believed is true, it means that there really is an Almighty God who not only was ruling over the world then, but is ruling over it now; it means there is a Jesus Christ who is Lord of all, that is, of all men and all things everywhere and always; it means that there is a Holy Spirit who can draw our splintered race together and can bestow upon mankind power to live a new kind of life.

A man's final conclusion about the credibility and the truth of these affirmations will not be reached simply by the inspection of historical evidences, though he must inspect and assess the historical evidences as honestly as he can. His conclusion will depend also on his attitude to the questions that I have discussed in the preceding lectures, about whether there is a personal God, who is in personal relations with mankind. If a man should have made up his mind that that is incredible before he examines the apostolic testimony, then he will be bound to conclude that the New Testament is at best 'the wonderful monument of an immense delusion', and his problem will be how to find an alternative to the Christian explanation of the facts. But even if you approach the apostolic testimony without any assumption that what it declares is incredible and cannot possibly be true, there are still serious difficulties in the way of reaching a conclusion about it, difficulties of which many simple and sincere Christian believers are unaware.

In the first place, there are no registers of births and deaths which we can inspect in order to satisfy ourselves when and where Jesus was born and died. The exact dates of his birth and death are, in fact, uncertain. Moreover, we have no strictly contemporary evidences concerning his earthly life. The earliest documents in the New Testament date from about twenty years after his death, and the earliest of the Gospels from thirty or forty years, though this no doubt incorporates matter which had been written down previously. A further difficulty is that there are no documentary evidences worth mentioning for the life of Christ which come from non-Christian sources.

These facts are not to be gainsaid, and they obviously give a handle to anyone who is inclined to say that the evidences for the existence of Jesus, or at any rate for reconstructing the story of his life, are neither contemporary nor disinterested enough to warrant positive conclusions. There have even been people who have advocated the negative conclusion that Jesus never really existed and is a purely mythical figure—a fantastic conclusion, no doubt, which has been adequately dealt with by non-Christian scholars on the extreme Left of biblical studies, like M. Loisy and M. Guignebert in France. The general conclusion of scholars who have devoted their lives to the study of the evidences is not only that Jesus is indubitably an historical figure, but that the New Testament enables us to form a sufficiently definite impression of his Person to justify the Christian belief in him, if on other grounds that belief is not held to be incredible. Scholarly opinion differs

D

about the extent to which it is possible from the Gospels to reconstruct an account of the actual course of events in any detail; there are, in particular, differences of opinion about whether or not the Gospel according to St. John contains genuine historical reminiscences. But with that qualification it can be confidently said that the most probable, indeed the only satisfactory, explanation of the evidences in the Gospels, when they have been rigorously scrutinized and sifted, is that the historic Jesus was the kind of Person that the apostolic testimony affirmed him to be. The idea is now discredited among scholars (though it popularly persists) that beneath the surface of the Gospels we can unearth a purely human prophet of the divine Fatherhood and human brotherhood who was transformed by St. Paul into a supernatural Saviour.

The objection may, of course, be raised that most of the scholars who devote themselves to the study of this subject, and who reach this conclusion, are Christian believers and even ordained ministers of a Christian church, who therefore have a life interest, and in the latter case an economic interest, in reaching the conclusion that they do reach. This again is true, and plainly Christians have a motive, which other people do not have, to concentrate their learning upon a study of Christian origins. Anyone, however, is at liberty to investigate the matter for himself. The claim is made, not that Christian belief about Jesus Christ should be accepted on the *ipse dixit* of any ecclesiastical authority or company of scholars, but that it is—I do not say necessitated by, but—congruous with the evidences that exist.

I should certainly allow that a church which anxiously disciplines and eventually excommunicates any of its theologians who reach heterodox conclusions about Christian origins, thereby diminishes the confidence we can have in the disinterestedness of their conclusions, for the only agreement worth having is that of men who possess the right to differ. But happily, most of the churches with which we have to do in this country, recognize that this is so and allow their theologians the liberty that they require in order to be free from the suspicion of cooking their conclusions.

My own misgiving about our New Testament scholars is not

that they are improperly prejudiced, nor that they are credulous, nor that they are too critical, but that they are too good, though I would add that there were more grounds for this misgiving before 1914 than there have been since. What I mean is that in order to understand the New Testament, a man needs to be alive in a world that is exposed to gales, both calamitous and glorious, like those that were blowing then, whereas too much New Testament criticism before 1914 was carried on by divines who were dealing with still-life in their studies. Concerning this, P. T. Forsyth, who was an outstanding exception to the rule, said: 'Often (just as a vast memory may impair the power of judgment) you find the finest critical faculty and the most powerful scholarly apparatus, conjoined with a moral nature singularly naïve, and beautifully simple and unequal to the actual world. Their experience of life and conscience has no record of lapse or shame. Their world is a study of still-life; it has not the drama, the fury, the pang, the tragedy, the crisis of the actual world at large, with its horrible guilt and its terror of judgment.'[4]

Since 1914 theologians, like other people, have been less inclined to look for a Jesus who was the author of moral precepts that would be harmless in a Sunday School, or of a programme of world evolution that comported easily with sanguine political expectations. There is no evidence whatever for the existence of a Jesus like that. All the same, we can trace in the New Testament a development in the interpretation of the Person and Work of Christ. St. Paul, the writer of the Epistle to the Hebrews, and the author of the books attributed to St. John, see more in, and more of, the Person and Work of Christ than the first three Gospels or the early chapters of the Acts of the Apostles and more even, so far as we can tell, than Jesus himself was conscious of, or at any rate spoke about, during his life on earth.

But this is what you would expect. The historic Christ was not primarily a teacher, but a Saviour; not a human prophet who came to give good advice but the eternal Son of God who came to deliver men from guilt by triumphing in and over death on their behalf, and so inaugurating a new creation of the race. This work of his could not be apparent, nor could it be taken in, till he had done it. It was only when Christ had finished the work that he came to do that its meaning and scope and implications could be got home. It was only after he had given himself to the utmost for the sins of the world and after God had raised him from the dead and he had ascended on high that he might fill all things—that these mighty acts could be publicly and intelligibly proclaimed, and what they had accomplished could be unfolded to the minds of believing men.

John Morley said that there are some books which cannot be adequately reviewed for twenty or thirty years after they come out.[5] It is no less true that there are some deeds which cannot be adequately interpreted, some persons whose work cannot be adequately evaluated, for at least as long. It will not then surprise us that the apostolic testimony to Christ and to the meaning of his work did not come forth full-blown on the very morrow of the cloud's taking him out of sight. The astonishing thing is not that the apostles realized so slowly, but that they realized so swiftly, what God had done to them and for the whole race of men in the work of Christ. The miracle is that within about sixty or seventy years the final word about the work of Christ had been spoken, the deepest insight had been attained, so that all the theology that has been written since the New Testament took shape has not really added anything to it but has been in the nature of a commentary upon it; and the longer a man lives with the New Testament the more sure he becomes that there is still further truth to break forth from it. 'How wonderful the gospel of Christ is!' exclaimed Dr. Dale. 'I have been thinking about it and preaching about it for more than forty years, and yet there seem to be vast provinces of truth in it which I am only just beginning to explore.' [6]

But there is another extraordinary thing. Although by the time the first three (or synoptic) Gospels were written, the apostolic testimony to the work of Christ, notably in St. Paul, had conveyed to the Christian mind the universal scope of Christ's work as the head of a new creation and its cosmic reach, yet those first three Gospels were not recast in the light of the fuller insight that had come. Although they have been affected by it in some degree, they reproduce with wonderful faithfulness the perspective, the point of view and the portraiture of Jesus and his disciples before the cross and resurrection had made all things new. Thus, with the synoptic gospels as a starting point, we are still able to map out the stages, albeit only approximately, by which Jesus, who in the first instance announced the impending fulfilment by God of his promises to Israel and the establishment of God's kingly rule over his people, came to be recognized after his death and resurrection as in his own Person both the fulfiller and the fulfilment of all those promises, and not least of that mysterious promise of a suffering servant of the Lord who was wounded because men had sinned . . . who shed his life-blood, and let himself be numbered among rebels, bearing the great world's sins, and so won the victory;[7] and how finally it was discerned that this Jesus was not only God's agent in redemption, not only God personally present rescuing mankind from guilt to holiness, restoring a disobedient race to obedience, but also that he had been from the first God's agent in creation, he in whom all things had originally cohered, and in whom at last all would be brought together again into unity and offered up as a worthy response of adoration to the creative love of the Eternal Father.

This final insight could not have been made explicit until Christ had done his central work in his passion and resurrection, and a generation or two had had time to assimilate and to reflect upon it, but it is congruous with all that we are told about him from the start. Either he was and is what the apostolic testimony proclaimed him to be, or it is impossible to find any coherent meaning in the whole New Testament and it must be given up as meaningless or unaccountable. It is between these two possibilities that a decision has to be made in the end. The first, as I have said, cannot be demonstrated, and the second does not ask to be.

As regards the question whether the full New Testament belief in Christ is consistent with what historical criticism allows us to affirm about the Jesus of history, I accept these words of Dr. Emil Brunner: 'Faith can be combined with all kinds of historical criticism which do not alter the historical image of the existence of Jesus to such an extent that—so far as faith is concerned—it would be impossible to understand the apostolic testimony to Christ'.[8] We certainly know less than we could wish to know about the historical image of the existence of Jesus, that is about his earthly life, but all that we do know, or all that a rigorous criticism of the evidences leaves us with, is consistent with the fully developed apostolic testimony. There is enough to warrant the decision of faith; there is not enough to necessitate it.

I come back here to the point with which I began to-day. Just as in nature and in his speaking through the prophets, God veils himself even in revealing himself so that men's minds are not coerced into acknowledging him, so too in his supreme revealing of himself in Christ, his eternal Son made man, God has left room for the exercise of a man's choice and decision—in a word, for the exercise of faith. For faith does not mean the acceptance of demonstrable propositions concerning intangible subjects. It means trust in a person. In the decision of faith a man commits himself beyond what the evidences necessarily require, as he does when he marries his wife. Faith means taking a risk, making a venture, and discovering in experience whether he, in whom you believe, is entitled to make that absolute claim upon the allegiance of your whole life that the apostolic testimony declares that he is entitled to make. Whatever may be the case with other creeds, Christian belief cannot be proved first and practised afterwards. The proof and the practice go hand in hand. All therefore that lectures on Christian belief can do is to show that it is not unreasonable to make the venture of faith; that a man who commits himself to faith in Christ is not committing intellectual suicide but is taking a step which may open his mind to the perception of truth and his soul to the experience of power, which otherwise he will miss.

I have not said anything about the miracles of Christ, and I do not intend to say much here.[9] Popular thought on this subject is much confused and a dictum like that of the late Sir Oliver Lodge that 'miracles lie all around us: only they are not miraculous' does not help to dispel the confusion. All I need say here is that, since no historical truths can be demonstrated, obviously miracles cannot be, and the attempt to prove the divinity of Christ by demonstrating the occurrence of his miracles was mistaken; the Gospels indeed show that Christ himself would have condemned it. On the other hand, there is no reasonable justification for the rationalist dogma, that miracles never happen, which Renan, for example, laid down in the preface to his *Vie de Jésus.* If Christ was what the apostolic testimony declares him to be, we cannot say in advance what he could or could not do. The only proper course is to weigh the evidences, and the man who is disposed to credit every wonder-story that is told about Christ is just as likely to go wrong as the man who refuses to believe that anything extraordinary happened. It is certainly congruous with belief in Christ as the Son of God and Regenerator of mankind, that the power of God to heal and restore and revive should have been present in him and that he should have wrought mighty acts. But it is also likely enough that legendary miracle-stories should have been subsequently affixed to him and the so-called apocryphal gospels show this process generously at work. There is a striking contrast, however, between the type of miracle that is attributed to Christ in the canonical gospels and those in the apocryphal gospels. There are few in the former that bear the familiar marks of legend, but it is neither possible nor necessary for a believer to draw a hard and fast line, and in certain cases he will be wise to suspend judgment. A believer, that is, a man who accepts the apostolic testimony to the miracle of Christ's Person and Work, will not, on the one hand, boggle at miracles as such, nor, on the other hand, will he fear that his faith is collapsing if he comes to the conclusion that, for instance, the discovery of the coin in the fish's mouth never actually occurred.

As Professor Dodd has said: 'the real problem for the student of the New Testament is not whether this or that incident in the life of Jesus is credibly reported, this or that saying rightly attributed to him. . . . It is whether the fundamental affirmations of the apostolic preaching are true and relevant.' [10] And there are more data that have yet to be taken into account before the question can be finally answered.

NOTES

[1] Cp. Paul Tillich, *The Shaking of the Foundations*, p. 89.

[2] In an address on Christmas Day 1931, reproduced in *Young India.*

[3] E. M. Forster's *Life of G. Lowes Dickinson*, p. 212.

[4] *The Person and Place of Jesus Christ*, p. 201.

[5] *Recollections*, i. 257.

[6] *Life of R. W. Dale*, p. 631.

[7] Isaiah 53 :5, 12.

[8] *The Mediator*, p. 168.

[9] I have discussed the subject in a booklet entitled *Miracles*, published by the Church Literature Association. See also Alan Richardson, *The Miracle Stories of the Gospels*.

[10] *The Apostolic Preaching and its Developments*, p. 186.

IV

THE HOLY SPIRIT

*

IT is a commonplace remark among theologians to-day that the doctrine of the Holy Spirit has been much neglected in the past, at any rate in Western Christendom, and that perhaps what is most needed in our time is a fresh and clear and comprehensive exposition of this doctrine. There are very many Christians to whom God the Father means something, and to whom Jesus Christ means something, but to whom the Holy Spirit means practically nothing. This is illustrated by the comparative importance that is popularly attached to the festivals of Christmas and Easter, on the one hand, and of Whitsun, on the other. Over twenty years ago Professor Raven said (and I apprehend he would have no grounds yet for retracting his words) that 'if we are not quite in the position of the group that St. Paul found at Ephesus, who "had not so much as heard whether there be any Holy Ghost", at least there is amongst us grave uncertainty as to His Person and Work.' [1]

Exactly a hundred years ago Frederick Denison Maurice wrote to his fiancée: 'I should like to be with you on Whit-Sunday; but this year we must be content to wish each other the infinite blessings of it at a distance. They seem to me more wonderful the more I think of them. Sometimes it seems as if they were the very root of all our life. I cannot but think that the reformation in our day, which I expect is to be more deep and searching than that of the sixteenth century, will turn upon the Spirit's presence and life.' [2] Although since then reformation in the church has been much spoken about, its coming tarries, and it may be that it tarries because of failure to look afresh and persistently at what is entailed in 'the Spirit's presence and life.'

Since Maurice's time a considerable number of books has been written about the doctrine of the Holy Spirit, but while many of them have valuable qualities, there is none of which one could say that it rings the bell. I have seen the suggestion made that no one can be expected to write a book—*a fortiori*, I suppose, to deliver a lecture—about the Holy Spirit, that will 'come off'. When the present Bishop of Bristol was writing his book on the subject, and it is a good book, he showed his manuscript to a friend who told him that he had undertaken an impossible task and that it is unfair to ask anyone to write a *real* book about the Spirit. [3]

What made his friend say that was probably the idea that to write or read a book about the Holy Spirit is like writing or reading a book about breathing. If you can breathe, you don't need a book; if you can't, a book won't help you. Obviously, there is something in that. It is saying, however, that books on such a subject are superfluous, not that they are impossible. If a man hasn't got any friends, books about friendship will not help him; but they can be written, and they are of value. In the present case, it seems to me that the source of the difficulty lies elsewhere. A great book, a bell-ringing book, about the Holy Spirit could be written, though it might be in the form of a poem or a novel rather than a theological treatise. The reason why this book has not yet been written is that conscious experience of the presence and life of the Spirit among contemporary Christians is so thin and weak and hampered[4] that conditions do not exist in which anyone can write with full-blooded conviction on the subject. It will be written not by an individual out of his own researches or mystical experience—not in the seclusion of a study or a cell—but by a member of a community which is making the corporate discovery of what it means to live and act and change the world in the power and freedom of the Spirit.

The best description of the Holy Spirit is that he is 'God in action in human life'.[5] There are quite a lot of people to-day who have some measure of conviction about a God who is more or less remotely over the world, and who have some conviction about Jesus Christ not only as the Great Exemplar but as an his-toric Saviour; but a sense of, and a conviction about, God actually present and active in the life of to-day is another matter and a rare thing. I don't, of course, deny that there are individuals who believe that they receive strength from the Holy Spirit to resist their temptations and to overcome their weaknesses and their fears. But, as we shall see, belief in the Holy Spirit does not mean merely that there is a source of spiritual invigoration available for individual persons, a heightening or releasing of their natural energies. If that were all it meant, we might as well recast the Lord's promise, 'Ye shall receive power when the Holy Ghost is come upon you', into 'Thou shalt receive power after that the psychoanalyst has done with you.' [6]

In the New Testament the presence and life of the Spirit are a corporate experience, a shared experience. No individual can recapture that experience by himself or for himself. It can be recaptured, or rather received again, only when men come out from their individual isolation or from their shelters in introverted groups and sects and parties, and when they come together on a common ground with nothing but the faith and expectancy of Christ's disciples. Meanwhile anything that is written or said about the Holy Spirit, if it is to be authentic, will point to a gift and an experience that we may hope to receive in full measure, but not to one that we surely possess or can describe as men who thoroughly know what they are talking about. At any rate, for my part I am bound to introduce what I am going to say with that confession.

I propose now, first, to direct your attention to what the Bible says about the Holy Spirit, and especially to the difference between what the Holy Spirit is represented as doing in the Old Testament and in the New. We shall then go on to consider what, according to Christian belief, is the permanent work of the Holy Spirit, and what are 'the fruits of the Spirit'.

The root meaning of the word that is translated 'spirit' in the Old Testament is wind or breath. It signifies the powerful, sweeping wind of the desert, not the gentle zephyr; and when used of breathing, it means not ordinary, quiet breathing, but agitated, violent breathing.[7] So it comes to signify any manifestation of strong, uncontrollable power. In the earlier stages of the Old Testament there is nothing particularly moral or holy in the conception of spirit, and it has affinities with what the South Sea Islanders know as *mana*, a mysterious, supernatural power or influence which can be tapped and used by a warrior or the chief of a tribe, for example. We haven't time to trace in detail the stages by which in the Old Testament this primitive conception was gradually transformed by being brought into relation with the All-holy God, the creator and redeemer.

As the Hebrews learned the relation in which they stood to God, his Spirit came to be thought of as the vital energy of the divine nature, God's exerting power. It was thought of as the source of vitality, particularly of the special gifts and endowments of outstanding men—for instance, as the source of artistic skill,[8] of heroism in war,[9] of wisdom in government.[10] Above all, the Spirit of God was the well-spring of the inspiration of the prophets, which enabled them to speak out boldly and clearly of the righteousness of God, of his judgment on national and personal sin, and of his promise of deliverance. In the Book of Hosea (9. 7) the prophet is described as 'the man that hath the spirit'. The work of the Holy Spirit was regarded as primarily an occasional, irregular, spasmodic output of the divine energy in human life, which from time to time took hold of individual men and raised them to an exceptional level of insight or activity beyond the scope of normal human capacity.

But before the close of the Old Testament period the conception of the work of the Spirit had been enlarged, and God was recognized as being invisibly present throughout the universe through his Spirit. 'Whither shall I go then from thy spirit? Or whither shall I flee from thy presence?'[11] In the first chapter of Genesis (which belongs to one of the latest strata in the Old Testament) the Spirit of God is represented as at the creation hovering or brooding over the face of the waters. God, it seems to say, creates by his Word, and by his Spirit vitalizes what he creates, so that the Spirit is the vitalizing energy of the cosmos. Thus the Spirit of God came to be looked upon as the source of all life, the life-giver, the giver of physical and psychical life.

Yet there is more than this in the Old Testament, by way of promise and expectation. Man needs more than vital energy in order to live as God designs that he should live; with that alone he may be as good as dead. The men who in the vision of Ezekiel (chap. 37) were likened to dry bones were alive in a sense, but in a profounder sense they were dead. Ezekiel's prophecy contains the promise that God can and will impart to these men, who are more dead than alive, a new kind of life, a new kind of relationship with himself and with one another (v. 22), a life that is pure and holy and obedient (v. 23), peaceful and fruitful (v. 26), and crowned with the divine blessing (v. 27). [12] Although in the Old Testament this higher kind of life is experienced and manifested by God's people only occasionally and at rare moments and chiefly in exceptional individuals, notably the prophets, still the promise is there that a time will come when it will be made available for all. 'Then shall it be that I pour out my spirit on all; your sons and daughters shall be inspired, your old men shall dream dreams, your young men shall see visions; even upon your slaves, both men and women, I will pour out my spirit in those days.' [13]

This promise was, according to Christian belief, fulfilled in the events to which the New Testament or the apostolic testimony bears witness. Because Jesus Christ is generally thought of as the main subject of the New Testament, it is easy to overlook the fact that the Holy Spirit is at least equally its subject. We can take only brief note of a few of the events in which the Holy Spirit is said to come with power and to do his reviving and renewing work.

At the beginning of St. Luke's Gospel, not only is Jesus conceived by the Holy Spirit, but also John the Baptist and his parents are filled with the Holy Spirit. These are, as it were, the first drops of the great shower or outpouring of Holy Spirit that is to descend upon mankind through the work of Christ and to make all things new. Then when Jesus was baptized in the River Jordan, 'the Spirit of God brooded a second time over the waters, to vivify a new creation by resting on the new Head of mankind'.[14] Throughout his ministry it is in the power of the Spirit that Jesus performs his mighty acts of healing and restoration, which are signs that a new age has dawned wherein God is going to bestow upon mankind wholeness and integrity. But during the incarnation, that is, during the life of Jesus in the flesh, these signs of the Spirit's presence and life were inevitably confined to Palestine, the little country to which the earthly ministry of Jesus was restricted. It was the death of Jesus which, as St. John's Gospel indicates, 'meant the setting free of the Holy Spirit for all.' [15] The Holy Spirit could be given in his fullness only when Jesus had been glorified by his crucifixion, resurrection, and exaltation to the throne of God. Christ ascended that he might fill all things, and now the Holy Spirit could be poured out upon all men, and his recreating work within mankind could be extended universally.

The day of Pentecost, as it is described in the Acts of the Apostles (chap. 2), signifies the inauguration of this universal outpouring and bestowing of vivifying power on all who would believe the good news about the new age that had begun. The important thing about Pentecost is not the strange, temporary phenomena that are said to have occurred, but the permanent transformation of human life that then began. As regards the more sensational phenomena—the rushing mighty wind, the tongues of fire, the sudden speaking (or hearing) in many languages—these are best understood as symbolic of the inner promise and potency of the event. The coming of the Spirit with power lit up the minds of Christ's disciples to see the real meaning of what he had taught and done, of his sufferings and his triumph. It changed them from disciples into apostles, from a group of perplexed individuals into a confident community with a single purpose. It impelled them to proclaim abroad with burning eloquence all that they had learned of the mighty acts of God. The linguistic miracle ('the gift of divers languages'), which tradition associates with Pentecost, but which doesn't make sense if taken as the prosaic record of a thing that actually happened then and there,[16] makes all the sense in the world if it is taken to symbolize the fact that henceforth it will be the work of the Holy Spirit to convey the good news of Christ to all nations and to enable all men to hear about 'the wonderful works of God'.

I do not mean to say that there were no extraordinary or abnormal occurrences in the primitive church. The outpouring of the Spirit resulted in a temporary effervescence as well as in the permanent transformation which remained when the effervescence had subsided. To the effervescence belongs the phenomenon known as 'glossolalia' or 'speaking with tongues', which is a familiar accompaniment of religious revivals and which is quite a different thing from speaking in foreign languages. St. Paul, who knew all about it, put this phenomenon in its right place (which he valued indeed more than we are likely to do) and firmly rebuked those who treated it as the thing that really mattered.[17]

The thing that really mattered was the new kind of common life for mankind which had sprung into existence since Pentecost and of which I tried to give you a rough sketch in Lecture III. Its characteristic quality was that kind of love that the New Testament calls *agape*, immortally delineated by St. Paul in the thirteenth chapter of the First Epistle to the Corinthians. *Agape* and its counterpart *eros* are Greek words that you will find frequently cropping up in current theological literature. Both are words that can be translated 'love', but 'love' is an unsatisfactory word since it covers all the types of affection that range from Hollywood to heaven. Nor was there a ready-made word in Greek that would express the kind of divine love which Christ had revealed, a love of the unlovely and unloveable, so different from that natural human love (*eros*) which is attracted only by desirable objects.[18] Therefore, the Christians took a little-used Greek word *agape* and appropriated it to God's love in Christ and to that love of their unlikeable brethren which the Holy Spirit imparted to them.

I will not repeat what I have said already about the characteristics of the Christian brotherhoods or communities which came into being around the Mediterranean world during the first century after Christ. The Christian belief is that these were the first-fruits of the new creation, vitalized by the Spirit of God; that here we have to do not with something that simply evolved out of the inherent potentialities of human nature, but with the creation of a new kind of personal relationship between God and man and of human beings one with another; and that this was due to the descent, the outpouring, let us say, to a new kind of activity, of the Holy Spirit, which the work of Christ had made possible. Let us inquire then what the difference was between the activity of the Holy Spirit before and after the coming of Christ.

The difference is not absolute. It is the same Holy Spirit who was active in human life before and after the coming of Christ. But the work of Christ issued in such an enlarging and enriching of the Spirit's activity that language was used[19] which implied that the Spirit was then given for the first time. Broadly speaking, we can say that after Pentecost his activity in human life was *inward* where before it had been outward, *permanent* where before it had been spasmodic, *corporate* where before it had been individual, and *universal* where before it had been national. Moreover and above all, he was now known to be the Spirit *of Christ* and so had a personal character and quality which before could not have been clearly perceived. Consider each of these points.

First, in the Old Testament, or under the old covenant, the will of God was made known to his people, on the one hand, through the outward ordinances of the Law or the Torah which laid down a comprehensive and coherent pattern of righteous social conduct appropriate to the peculiar circumstances of the Hebrew nation, and, on the other hand, through the utterances of the prophets who were moved by the Spirit to speak out concerning the will of God in particular contingencies of affairs. The Law in its main principles was good,[20] but the trouble with social or personal life that is regulated by external ordinances is that these tend to be more and more elaborated until complete compliance with them becomes not only intolerably burdensome but impossible, and so the attempt to comply with them becomes a source of frustration. This we call 'legalism'. Legalism is the going bad of a thing that in itself is good and necessary. The legalism of Judaism in the period before the coming of Christ was the more hopeless because the voice of prophecy, which would have challenged and reformed it, had for a long time been stilled.

Nevertheless, the hope was maintained even through this period that God would resolve his people's predicament by again speaking prophetically,[21] and above all by inwardly transforming them through the activity of his Spirit so that they would do his will freely and spontaneously, no longer as a matter of external or legal constraint. Jeremiah had uttered this promise. 'Behold a day comes, saith the Lord, when I will make a fresh covenant with all Israel . . . I will put my law within them, and write it on their hearts . . . no longer shall they have to teach their fellows, each instructing each how to know the Lord; for they shall all know me, both great and small.' [22] This promise was fulfilled in the coming of Christ. He was a prophet (though much more than a prophet) sent by God to challenge and reform the Law, and the Holy Spirit brought about in those who yielded to him the inner transformation that Jeremiah had foretold.[23] The Christians of the apostolic age received a liberation from the bondage of the Law. They were emancipated from legalism. And this has been a mark of every great revival in the history of the church. For the church, as we shall see, has been prone to return to new forms of the bondage from which in principle it has been delivered.

Secondly, in the Old Testament the activity of the Spirit in human life was regarded as occasional or spasmodic, but in the New Testament he is the very presence and life of God in which believers live and move and have their being. He comes now not, as it were, in occasional gusts or cloudbursts, but as a steady shower or an unfailing spring of water or a constant breeze. As water is a perpetual source of new life in the earth or as a breeze gives energy where otherwise there would be lassitude, so the Holy Spirit is the permanent source of all spiritual life and energy in mankind. It is highly significant, and easily overlooked, that in the New Testament the Christians do not pray for the coming of the Spirit.[24] The Christians live in the Spirit; it is he who enables them to pray. They have not to call down an absent Spirit, but only to recall that they have once for all been received into a relationship with God, which means that they permanently have the Spirit in the depths of their being if not on the surface of their consciousness. Prayers for the coming of the Spirit, which are often used by Christians now, can no doubt be interpreted consistently with this, but they are liable to mislead. The Collect for Whit-Sunday in the Book of Common Prayer strikes the right note. 'Let us remind ourselves' of this or that is one of the commonest clerical clichés. It is often used about things of which people have never heard before and so of which they cannot 'remind themselves'. But it is precisely what Christians should say about their being in the Spirit. They need only to be still and know that he is the present and permanent source of all their life and to rejoice in his strength.

Thirdly, we saw that in the Old Testament the Holy Spirit was regarded primarily as an occasional output of divine power which took hold of individuals and intermittently raised them to an exceptional level of insight or activity. But in the New Testament the primary work of the Holy Spirit is to create and sustain a

E

common or corporate life, a life in community, 'God's co-opera-
tive society.'[25] The New Testament word for this is *koinonia*.
When the risen Lord took leave of his disciples he forbade them
to separate till they had received the promise of the Father,[26] and
it was when 'they were all together in one place'[27] that power
from on high descended on them and welded them into a community which was of one heart and soul and had all things in
common.[28] The inspiration of individuals is now subordinate to,
and a consequence of, this common life in the Spirit. This did not
mean that individuality or personal gifts were suppressed or forced
into a rigid uniformity of exercise. On the contrary, they receive
a freer and fuller exercise within the concordant life of the community. 'All these are inspired by one and the same Spirit, who
apportions to each one individually as he wills.'[29]

It has been said, perhaps with a shade of exuberance, that 'the
community or fellowship of the Spirit is neither a drab mono-
tone, nor a clash of opposites; rather is it a revelation of a brilliant
variety of colours, which are blended together in a perfect harmony. . . . The Christian society is not a machine, nor a mere
conglomeration of atoms, but a living unity of inter-relationships
in which every member has a part to play in the service of the
whole and is indispensable to the health of the whole.'[30] That, no
doubt, somewhat exaggerates what was actually realized even in
the apostolic age, but that is the kind of thing that happened, and
nothing of that fashion had been experienced before. Hence the
winning, expansive power of the apostolic church. Hence, too,
the appropriateness of the metaphor of the body and of similar
metaphors that were applied to the church. The metaphor of the
body is applied in more than one way, but most illuminating is
the idea of Christ as the Head, who is exalted in the heavenly
places where he is the principle of universal unity. The Christians
(and all men by vocation) are members of Christ's body, each
with his own indispensable function, whether conspicuous or
inconspicuous. The Holy Spirit is the vital power who circulates
throughout the body and in whom all the members share. It is a
great mistake therefore, to think of the Holy Spirit as a power
that is, or can be, imparted to individuals in isolation. To receive
the Holy Spirit is to be drawn out of isolation into the fellowship

the common life, of the body of Christ which is animated by the Holy Spirit. Here, if anywhere, it is true that things have to be shared in order to be fully possessed.

Fourthly, in the Old Testament, the personal activity of the Holy Spirit is thought of as a prerogative of Israel, though this is not, of course, to say that he was really inactive in other nations before Christ came. Whatever its final scope and implications, the ministry of Jesus on earth was restricted to Israel, apart from a few exceptional incidents (which were naturally regarded after-wards as of much significance). Moreover, at Pentecost, despite the universal symbolism of which we took note, the Gospel was proclaimed only to Jews, and at first only Jews were received into the fellowship of the church. It was the Holy Spirit who taught the apostles, notwithstanding their inevitable prejudices, that the Christ was the Head, not of one nation only, but of all nations—the Head of mankind, and that his healing and restoring work was for the benefit of all nations. After a sharp struggle, however, the painful lesson was faithfully learned, and soon the way was clear for the Holy Spirit to draw men and women into the new creation, into the body of Christ, simply on the ground of their humanity and without respect to whether they had the correct physical or ecclesiastical pedigree. In retrospect, it seems plain that Christ came to draw all men unto him, and to bind all together in a universal community, whatever their nationality or race or class, but it was by no means clear to the earliest believers. It was the Holy Spirit who made it clear not only in theory, but in fact.[31]

The last and conclusive difference between belief in the Holy Spirit before and after the coming of Christ is that since Pente-cost he has been known to be the Spirit *of Christ*. In the fellowship or communion of the Spirit, men are brought not into tune with an impersonal infinite but into a personal relationship with Christ their Head. 'The Holy Spirit comes not so much to supply the absence of Christ as to accomplish His presence in the world as its Saviour and New Life.'[32] The work of the Holy Spirit is to continue, to implement, and to bring home to all men what Christ did for mankind once for all in his passion and resurrec-tion. It is the work of the Holy Spirit to bring illumination to all men, to convict them of their sinfulness or egocentricity, to convince them that in Christ, the Head of the race, the righteousness and *agape* of the Eternal God have been once for all made available to everyone who repents and believes the Gospel.

The Holy Spirit is the interpreter of Christ. He gradually unfolds more and more of the meaning of Christ's universal work for the race. In St. John's Gospel, Christ is represented as saying: 'I have yet many things to say to you, but you cannot bear them now. When the Spirit of truth comes, he will guide you into all the truth,' [33]—that is, into the inexhaustible truth that was concretely and concisely summed up in the historic work of Christ. The Holy Spirit has been doing this ever since, where men have been attentive and responsive to his guidance, and still the greatest saints and divines will acknowledge that they are only at the beginning of comprehending the wonderful works of God. Because the Holy Spirit is the Spirit of Christ there can be no excuse now for confusing him with *mana*, with weird impersonal manifestations of psychic energy, with ideological dynamism, or with vague mystical sentiments. 'Do not believe every spirit', we read, 'but test the spirits whether they are of God . . . by this you know the Spirit of God: every spirit which confesses that Jesus Christ has come in the flesh is of God, and every spirit which does not confess Jesus is not of God.' [34] 'Inspiration' as such is not a criterion of truth. Claims to inspiration must be tested by the character and teaching of Christ, by the ways of God's working which he has revealed, and by the witness of the apostolic testimony. 'That a thing is called spiritual,' said St. Augustine, 'is not always to be taken for praise.' [35] You shall know them by their fruits.

What more can be said of 'the fruits of the Spirit?' Much every way. Here are a few further indications of the kind of thing that the Holy Spirit does for persons and for communities of persons. He harmonizes and unifies. The individual man by nature, or left to himself, is subject to a welter of conflicting impulses, good, bad and indifferent. He is drawn, perhaps torn, this way and that and at the same time.[36] The more full a man is of sheer animal vitality, the greater the turmoil within. In the extreme case he is like the man in the Gospel who, when asked his name, called himself 'legion'. There are so many names by which I might be called

—idealist, realist, Don Juan, Don Quixote, devil, saint—that I know not which is the real 'I'. As Jesus brought the man to his right mind and unified his personality, so it is the work of the Holy Spirit to give health and harmony and singleness of mind to all men so that their varying impulses, ambitions and desires are brought into captivity to Christ their Head, subject to his all-embracing purpose and direction.

Likewise, any group of persons, assembled to face some problem or to undertake some enterprise, comes together with all sorts of conflicting prejudices, passions and insights. Unison may of course be imposed on them by the compulsive self-assertion of the strongest will. It is the work of the Holy Spirit, on the other hand, to bring a community, even a committee, to one mind by a free and candid interchange of thought and a pooling of all the resources of insight, criticism and goodwill that its members possess. The Holy Spirit does not turn men or societies out with mechanical uniformity like ninepins from a lathe. He enables men to become themselves, each with a distinct character and *attrait*, and to find themselves completed in a community of persons. Thus a man discovers, in the words of the American theologian Du Bose, that 'truth is not an individual thing; no one of us has all of it—even all of it that is known. Truth is a corporate possession, and the knowledge of it is a corporate process.' [37]

But men never attain in this world to a final harmony or completion. To live here is to move, to learn, to change. Both individuals and institutions, however, are always being tempted to settle down, to close their minds, to become petrified. 'I hate to meet a man whom I have known ten years ago,' said Benjamin Jowett, 'and find that he is at precisely the same point, neither moderated, nor quickened, nor experienced, but simply stiffened.' [38] It is the work of the Holy Spirit to disturb a man or an institution that is becoming settled or stiff; to break up what was taken for a fixed philosophy of life or a satisfactory routine of habit, in order that he may build up something further and better. The Holy Spirit works like an acid on all complacency. He points and presses men onwards into the unknown. 'It is good once in a while,' said Kierkegaard, 'to feel oneself in the hands of God, and not always and eternally slinking around the familiar nooks and corners of a town, where one always knows a way out.' [39] This too, is a fruit of the Spirit.

Lastly, it is the work of the Holy Spirit to humble and fortify mankind, and to fortify by humbling. 'Deliver me, O Lord,' prayed an old divine, who was both wise and good, 'from the errors of wise men; yea, and of good men.' [40] The Holy Spirit puts down the mighty from their thrones, the mighty in intellect and the mighty in virtue, as well as the mighty in power. It has been said that the favourite words of Jesus would seem to have been the 'last', the 'least', and the 'lost'. A man cannot persuade himself, but it is a favourite work of the Holy Spirit to persuade him, that he is the last, and the least, and the lost. The Holy Spirit can keep great men aware of their perilous condition, and show them that they are strong only when they confess their weakness. Who else can do that?'

I am not able in this course of lectures to include one on the doctrine of the Holy Trinity, but I hope it is the watermark which anyone who looks closely will see in all that I am saying. I may, however, in concluding this lecture just point out that the word 'person' in the expression 'Three Persons in one God' does not mean what is ordinarily meant by 'a person', that is, an individual centre of consciousness. One of the disadvantages under which a theologian labours is that he has so often to explain that the words he uses do not mean what they will naturally be taken to mean, although indeed theologians have no monopoly of this disadvantage. The use of the term 'Persons' in the doctrine of the Trinity has a singularly involved history, as all who study the development of Christian dogma know very well. All that need be said here is that the three 'Persons' in the Godhead are not like three separate human individuals: that would be tritheism. It would be nearer the truth to say that the doctrine of the Trinity means 'one God existent in and manifested under three eternal modes or aspects of being'.[41] If some bright theological student tells you that is 'Sabellianism', you may instruct him to hold his peace, for Sabellius held that the three aspects were purely temporary or economic. Nevertheless, these terms are not satisfactory either. Although all sorts of analogy, from clover to the triangle, have been brought into service, none properly meets the case and it is not to be expected that any should. Fortunately, it is possible for men who pray and worship to know the One God as Father, Son and Holy Spirit, without being able to comprehend the doctrine of the Trinity. The true, or at any rate the normal, pattern of Christian prayer is not prayer *to* Christ or the Holy Spirit, but prayer *to* God the Father of all *through* Jesus Christ, the Head of the race *in* the uniting power of the Holy Spirit.

NOTES

[1] C. E. Raven, *The Creator Spirit*, p. 1.

[2] *Life of F. D. Maurice*, i. 543.

[3] F. A. Cockin, *The Holy Spirit and the Church*, p. 96.

[4] See an article by P. N. Pare on 'The Doctrine of the Holy Spirit in the Western Church' in *Theology*, August 1948, pp. 293–300.

[5] F. W. Dillistone, *The Holy Spirit in the Life of To-day*, p. 25.

[6] N. Micklem, *The Creed of a Christian*, p. 140.

[7] See N. Snaith, *I Believe In . . .*, p. 95.

[8] Exodus 36:1f.

[9] Judges 13:25, 14:6.

[10] 1 Kings 3:28.

[11] Psalm 139:7.

[12] See Dillistone, op. cit., p. 41.

[13] Joel 2:28f.

[14] H. B. Swete, *Hastings' Dictionary of the Bible*, ii. 406.

[15] R. H. Strachan, *The Fourth Gospel*, p. 228. Cp. A. Loisy, *Le Quatrième Evangile*, pp. 882f.; Sir Edwyn Hoskyns, *The Fourth Gospel*, p. 633.

[16] See A. Loisy, *Les Actes des Apôtres*, pp. 186–191.

[17] 1 Corinthians 13 and 14.

[18] Too rigid a distinction can, however, be drawn between *agape* and *eros*: see J. Burnaby, *Amor Dei*, pp. 15ff.

[19] E.g. John 7:39.

[20] On the whole subject of the Law of God, see my book *Christ's Strange Work*.

[21] Malachi 3:1, 4:5f., Deuteronomy 18:18, Acts 3:22.

[22] Jeremiah 31:31, 33f.
[23] Cp. 2 Corinthians 3:3–6.
[24] Cp. O. C. Quick, *Doctrines of the Creed*, p. 282. Luke 11:13 is an exception that proves the rule; in Matthew's version of the saying (7:11) there is no reference to the Holy Spirit.
[25] The title of a book by C. L. Marson.
[26] Acts 1:41.
[27] Acts 2:1.
[28] Acts 2:44; 4:32.
[29] 1 Corinthians, 12:11.
[30] Dillistone, op. cit. p. 76.
[31] See e.g. Acts 10:44f.
[32] C. Gore, *The Holy Spirit and the Church*, p. 110.
[33] John 16:12f.
[34] 1 John 4:1ff.
[35] *Homilies on St. John*, p. 719.
[36] Cp. pp. 31f. *supra*.
[37] W. P. Du Bose, *Turning Points in my Life*, p. 56.
[38] *Life and Letters*, 1:414.
[39] *Journals*, p. 97.
[40] D. Butler, *The Life and Letters of Robert Leighton*, p. 520.
[41] Raven, op cit., pp. 26f.; Cockin, op. cit., pp. 51f.

V

THE CHURCH

*

MATTHEW ARNOLD'S saying[1] that men cannot do without Christianity and that they cannot do with it as it is acquires more point if for 'Christianity' we read 'the church'. That men cannot do without the church seems to be shown not only by the tenacious, if distant, hold that it keeps on multitudes who would be considerably embarrassed if they had to explain why the church exists at all—nor only by a curious nostalgia or wistful interest that is felt, if not acknowledged, by men who have either left the church or have never been inside it. It is shown also by the constant and pathetic clamour from outside that the church should give a lead about this or that or everything, and by the public sense of grievance that the church is not what it might be or ought to be.

For, on the other hand, it is equally plain that men cannot do with the church as it is. Here we must discriminate. The church, even as it is, gives creditable as well as discreditable offence. There is that in all men which cannot do with what the church stands for, and always has stood for in one way or another. Beneath everything in the church that bores and is stale, that depresses and distracts, it is difficult for men to escape the memory that it bears a witness that they would like to have hushed up. For there is that in every individual and in every human association which resents the disconcerting and exclusive claim that a Holy God makes to the obedience of all men and of the whole race. There is that in all of us which resents the disturbing affirmation that in Jesus Christ there has been a final act of judgment on every man and on every human institution, and a new creation apart from which men cannot be saved. We wanted only to go on exploring the old creation, and to express ourselves in terms of that. There is that in us which resents the uncanny assertion that there is present and active in the human conscience the Spirit of a Holy God, who is pressing upon us when we would be left to

71

ourselves, who is pressing us towards a way of common life in which we shall everywhere be responsible (not to the State nor to the will of a majority but) to an authority above all human authorities, and everywhere too responsible for one another, when all we wanted was to mind our own business and to pursue our own noble or sordid or dreamy enterprises.

To this we shall come back. But this is not what Matthew Arnold had in mind, nor is it what men to-day mostly mean when they say, or leave unsaid, that they cannot do with the church as it is. Men, at their best, cannot do with the church as it is, not because it bears a witness to the things of which I have just spoken, but precisely because it does not bear a clear and consistent witness to them. Men connect the church, not with the disturbing and renewing encounter of a Holy God, but, as someone has said, with 'unattractive services, tedious homilies, the smell of hymn-books, the petty round of ecclesiastical functions, the collection bag, an oppression due to lack of oxygen, and memories of Sunday-school.' [2]

And there is worse than that. The church makes large and lofty claims which are neutralized and even made to look absurd by its own condition and its feeble practice. It claims to have received a divine commission and to possess the secret of community; but in a period like this when immense social changes are taking place and immeasurable disasters threaten—when, if there is a body commissioned to speak plainly in God's Name, it could be sure of a hearing—no plain word is forthcoming, but only what sound like shrill archaisms or platitudes. So far from displaying the winning secret of community, the church, that is, the churches and the sects, cannot reconcile themselves one with another, let alone reconcile the world. So the grave question must be firmly asked whether the church is anything but an institution like gothic or gothic-revival architecture which still survives from a civilization that is rapidly passing away—an institution which has not yet been replaced but will be replaced, and which meanwhile retains an attraction for such men as have a nostalgia for the past, or as are without the courage or imagination to adapt themselves to the present and the future.

It is against the background of that heavy question that the nature of the church must be considered. What, according to Christian belief, is the church? Here, as throughout, when I say 'according to Christian belief' I should add in parenthesis 'so far as I can see'. I readily grant that other Christians may be able to see further than I, and you can sit at their feet or read their writings, when you will. My office here is neither to condemn nor to advertise the church or the churches, but to put before you what strikes me as the salient information that you ought to take into account in reaching your own conclusions.

I begin then by observing that the church is a subordinate object of Christian belief. This is not my idea, but that of the creeds, where belief in the church is affirmed quite a long way down. The Christian man fundamentally believes in, places his confidence in, God—in God the Father, in Jesus Christ, in the Holy Spirit. His belief in the church, or what he believes about the church, is (or ought to be) a corollary or consequence of his belief in God. You may possibly meet ardent churchmen who say they believe in God on the authority of the church, or who seem to be more concerned about the church or their church or even about ecclesiastical millinery and other trivialities than about the will of God for the church. But they do not know their stuff. There have always been men who, in a pregnant phrase quoted by T. H. Green, 'make religion their God instead of God their religion'.[3] That is a temptation to which every religious man is exposed; and it is a temptation of the devil.

In particular, I call your attention to the fact that, according to the creeds, belief in the church is subordinate to, and dependent upon, belief in the Holy Spirit. It is as fatal as it is common, in thinking about the church, to by-pass the Holy Spirit. For the Holy Spirit is the creator of the church, its Lord and Life-giver, its reformer and tormentor, and at last its only resource. I guess, in fact I do more than guess, that the divisions among Christians, between and across all the denominations, are due at bottom or for the most part to whether or not they take seriously and think through persistently the dependence of the church on the Holy Spirit; or, to say the same thing in another way, different beliefs about the church are rooted in different beliefs or unbeliefs about the Holy Spirit. Hence the importance for our subject to-day of what I tried to set forth in the preceding lecture about the Holy Spirit. To that also we shall come back.

To get at the root of the matter we must turn to what the Bible, and especially the apostolic testimony, says about the church. The Bible is the record of God's dealings with a people, a community of persons, and only secondarily with individuals, and then always within the context or framework of his relationship with his people. An idea of cardinal importance is that of the *covenant* that God makes with his people. The remote origins of this idea are obscure and debatable, but in its developed form, as articulated by the prophets of Israel, it means something different from what in common parlance to-day we mean by a covenant. We mean by a covenant a business transaction or a legal agreement between two equal parties. It is in the nature of a bargain. In the Bible the covenant is the free, unmerited and wholly gracious act of God by which he binds himself in a personal relationship with a people for whom he makes himself responsible, and who will enjoy the blessings of this relationship in so far as they respond to God's initiative.

'The idea is,' says Professor Dodd, 'that God, the Eternal King of the Universe, intervenes in human affairs to set up a certain enduring relation of a unique character between Himself and those men who will accept His terms . . . a relation going beyond that fundamental creaturely relation which all His works necessarily bear to their Creator.'[4] According to the Old Testament, the community which stands in this covenant-relation to God is first a family, then a tribe or collection of tribes, and finally a nation that is also a church. Just at what point in the history of Israel this people became aware of its covenant-relationship with God, we cannot be sure. It was the prophets of Israel, inspired by the Spirit of God, who drew out its meaning and, in the light of the prophetic teaching, the early history of the nation was interpreted in terms of this relationship.

Thus the people of Israel came to see that from the beginning of their national existence, God on his part had been creating, sustaining, guiding, calling, chastening and delivering them, whereas they on their part, had continually failed and refused to respond to the obligations of the covenant-relationship. They also came to see that God's covenant with them was not one of exclusive favouritism, but that the special relationship which he had established with them was for the sake of all nations, and in the last analysis arose out of God's eternal relationship to mankind. So in the Genesis mythology, God is represented as establishing his covenant with Noah and all his descendants,[5] that is, with the whole human race. The covenant was not a peculiar prerogative of Israel, but a truth with which they were entrusted for conveyance to the race.

But along with this deeper insight into the meaning and scope of the covenant-relationship went a sense of its inconclusiveness as it had so far been realized and of the impossibility of its fulfilment without some further intervention and recreative act of God. So the Old Testament points forward to, and contains the promise of, a new covenant and a universal community brought into personal relations with God. I have previously spoken of the promise of the new covenant in Jeremiah, chapter 31;[6] notice now the promise, in Isaiah, chapter 35, of the feast that God will make in which all nations are to participate. This symbolic image of a universal feast or banquet entered deeply into the Gospel of Jesus and his apostles.[7]

These promises, and all the promises of God, were in principle fulfilled in the New Testament, by the inauguration of the new covenant, though their final consummation lies beyond the sphere of history. Christ was not the founder of a church, or of Christianity, as is sometimes said; he is nowhere so described in the New Testament. The Person and the Work of Christ are the foundation of a recreated and reconstituted church, of a universal community in a new covenant-relationship with God. There was a church, a people of God, before Christ came; but that church was provisional, incomplete, inconclusive. The coming of Christ did not begin the church, but broke and remade the church that already existed. In him, the Son of God and Son of Man, there came at last a man, the Man, the new Adam, who perfectly responded to God's covenant, who completely obeyed the Father's will, even to the death of the cross. His death was the end of the old order and the beginning of the new.

It was the Holy Spirit who taught the apostles to see that the

crucifixion of Jesus, which seemed at first the greatest crime and
calamity that there had ever been, was really the event in which
the wickedness of men once for all encountered both the righteousness of the New Man and also the unfathomable love (*agape*)
of God, and that what looked like the final defeat of God's purpose was really the condition of its final triumph. Locked up in
the crucifixion were all the mysteries of God's love for the world,
and of man's unspeakable ingratitude, and of God's determina-
tion, notwithstanding, to win mankind not by compulsion but
by sacrifice. On the eve of his passion at the last supper, which was
a sacrificial feast, Jesus took a cup of which all drank and said,'This
is my blood of the (new) covenant, which is poured out for;many.'[8]
His blood, that is his life, offered to the Father on behalf of mankind was to inaugurate the new covenant-relationship for all men.

The cross, it has been said, is 'the point where God and Man,
Time and Eternity, Nature and Conscience, Judgment and Grace
meet for a new Creation.'[9] Because that is so, Christians have
gone on finding more and more meaning in the cross. It was the
act of God, of God in Manhood, of God with men, to which
everything led up and from which everything followed. It was
an end which was also a beginning, a death which was also the
spring of new life.

In lecture VI I shall have more to say about the cross in relation to
atonement and the forgiveness of sins. Here we take note of the
fact that this act of God in Christ, in which he reconciled the world
unto himself, was the foundation of the reconstituted church.
The founder of Christ's church, if we are to use that term, was
the Holy Spirit. It was the Holy Spirit, proceeding from the
Father and the Son, who formed and bound together and gave
insight and power to the new community of which Christ was
the living and exalted Head. The Holy Spirit, since he is not a
mere emanation from God but God himself present and active in
human life, is able to create this new kind of community in which
all men can be brought into a fully personal relationship with God
and with one another. It is a community which had from the start
an endless capacity for expansion and development, because it is
the community of the Holy Spirit who is active throughout the
world in hidden as well as in open ways.

It is not the church considered in itself or as a fixed institution that has the secret of all community life, but the Holy Spirit, the Lord and Life-giver, who can counteract and overcome the tendency of all institutions (not least ecclesiastical institutions) to become fixed, inflexible, and tied up inextricably with the cultures in which they originate or with which they are identified. I have spoken in the two preceding lectures of the characteristics of the community of the Holy Spirit as it sprang into existence in the first century of Christ's era. We shall do best now to consider and reflect upon certain aspects of the church's life as it spread out into history both in space and time. Note however that, according to Christian belief, the community of the Holy Spirit, of mankind drawn into the new covenant-relationship with God, is not confined to the church visible on earth. The greater part of it is no longer in this world, but where Christ is, delivered from the limitations of earthly existence. This is the cloud of invisible witnesses by which the church on earth is surrounded, all looking towards the final consummation when all things shall have been subjected to Christ, so that God may be everything to every one.[10]

Nor is the community of the Holy Spirit here on earth confined to those who are visibly members of the church or of one of the churches. The church visible (which is what I shall henceforth mean by 'the church'), that is, 'the whole congregation of Christian people dispersed throughout the whole world',[11] has not got a monopoly of the Holy Spirit. It is the mission of the church to be the visible and audible witness to a common life in the Spirit that is now available for all men, and to be the definite, open, publicly recognizable incorporation of that common life. But the Holy Spirit is already active in human life, where he is not yet definitely, openly or publicly acknowledged and confessed.

His hidden work is more pervasive than his open work. All that draws men together in their families and nations, all that moves them to work together in industry and trade, in the social services, in schools and universities, is the hidden work of the Holy Spirit, whereas it is men's individual and collective egotism, their setting of their own or sectional interests before the common good, that produce all the discord, division and injustice that blight the human scene. The pressures and tumults of egotism would carry men to sheer chaos and destruction, were not the Holy Spirit ever at work drawing men together who would keep themselves apart, moving them to co-operate despite their individual passions and ambitions, weaving order out of disorder, ordering 'the unruly wills and affections of sinful men', as a well-known prayer has it.

The church, in addressing mankind, is not looking towards alien territory, for the Holy Spirit has already been at work there before any churchmen came upon the scene. The church when it arrives is not bringing a message of which men have no intimation whatever in their previous experience. The church brings to mankind the good news that all the aspirations after truth, beauty and goodness which men experience compounded with very different aspirations, and all those movements towards fellowship and unity, harmony and integrity, which struggle with men's egocentric passions, are not unaccountable whims, but are the work of the Spirit of God within and among them, prompting them to become what by the divine constitution of their being they are, members one of another with one universal Head in whose will is peace. 'See here,' wrote William Law, 'the beginning and glorious extent of the *Catholic Church* of Christ, it takes in all the world. It is God's unlimited universal mercy to all mankind; and every human creature, as sure as he is born of *Adam*, has a birth of the Bruiser of the Serpent within him, and so is infallibly in covenant with God through Jesus Christ.' [12]

Thus the church is the community in which men know and confess what they are, and can become what they are—members of Christ, children of God, and inheritors of the kingdom of heaven. In the church men are brought together to confess the one God and Father of all, and Jesus Christ the Head of their race, and the Holy Spirit the creator of universal community.

In order that the church may serve this divine purpose, and bring this definite and distinct news to mankind, it must itself be a definite and distinct community, and indeed an exclusive community. 'A Gospel which is not exclusive will never include the world,' said P. T. Forsyth. 'No religion will include devotees which does not exclude rivals. Half Gospels have no dignity, and no future.' [13] Hence the distinct marks, signs or ordinances (the Word and the sacraments) which the church has jealously guarded and guards still, despite all the controversy and misunderstanding to which they have given rise. Without its distinct message and without its distinct bonds of membership the church would long ago have been merged and lost to sight in the ocean of society or in States that are always eager to absorb any *imperium in imperio*. Then the church would have ceased to bear that witness, which God designs it to bear, to and for society and the State. Thus it is for the sake of making a clear impact on the mind of the race, and it is in the interest of its universal mission, that the church must be definitely organized and have a palpable structure and ethos, and even be scrupulous about appearances. 'No public body can afford to live in its shirtsleeves, and pick up its meals, to disregard its social ritual and live casually.' [14]

A description of the church which would, I believe, be accepted by Christians generally, though it would, of course, be variously amplified by different denominations and theological schools, is this: 'The visible Church of Christ is a congregation of faithful men, in which the pure Word of God is preached, and the Sacraments duly administered.' [15] That brings out the fact that the preaching of the Word of God and the administration of the Sacraments are the chief distinguishing marks of the church as a visible community. I will try to explain why these marks of the church are important, and also why they have been misunderstood and their use perverted.

The Word of God in this context means the Gospel, the good news of God which has its centre and sum in the Person and Work of Christ. The Word of God is not a fixed or dead form of words. It means that the living God has spoken to mankind once for all in Christ as judge and deliverer—once upon a time, but also once for all. The Word of God spoken in Christ is made audible and actual to men in every age by the Holy Spirit who is the interpreter of Christ. Preaching, rightly understood, means not preaching about Christ, in the sense of merely recalling the character or teaching of an historical figure, but speaking in such a way that the Holy Spirit can make audible and bring home the Word of God, which is Christ himself, to the minds and consciences of contemporary men and women. The church, therefore, must attach great importance to preaching. 'How are men

F

to call upon him in whom they have not believed? And how are they to believe in him of whom they have never heard? And how are they to hear without a preacher?'[16]

But the church must also attach unique importance to the Bible and the creeds, since they contain the permanent message that the Holy Spirit has to interpret to all men and that the church has to deliver in all the languages of mankind, which include ever-changing forms of thought and so require much more than simple translation. The Bible is not itself the Word of God. It is a library of books, which records the course or complex of events in which the Word of God was once for all spoken in Christ's Person and Work, events which the Holy Spirit enabled prophets and apostles truthfully to interpret at the time. The message of the Bible comes to a head in what we have been calling the apostolic testimony, which is summarized and safeguarded in the creeds, notably in the Apostles' and Nicene creeds, though there were many other similar creeds in use in the ancient church. The creeds are thus a criterion by which one can tell whether any particular church or preacher is indeed preaching the Word of God or 'a different Gospel.'[17] They are also an outward, audible and venerable means by which men in all ages can express both their corporate response to the Word of God and their personal faith in Christ.

The proclamation of the Gospel or the Word of God is the concern and duty of all Christians, as is also that diligent and open-minded study of the Bible and the creeds without which proclamation of the Gospel becomes stale and partial and static. But to this end it is also requisite that certain men—and women, though that seems to be disputed—shall be set apart or ordained to make this proclamation and this study the main work of their lives. This is one reason for the existence of an ordained ministry in the church. 'The existence of a professional ministry,' it has been said, 'witnesses that a Gospel for life must issue in a life for the Gospel.'[18]

The other chief distinguishing mark of the church as a visible community is the administration of the sacraments. The sacraments are social actions through which the Holy Spirit draws men into the church and seals their membership, sustains them in its fellowship and welds them into unity. 'Plainly,' wrote William Temple, 'in a world of many languages the unity of the Church is better expressed and fostered by a common act than it could ever be by forms of words.'[19] Washing with water and eating bread and drinking wine are actions that are everywhere the same and can be universally understood whatever the language that accompanies their use.

The rite of initiation into the church is called baptism. In some traditions it is divided into two parts, baptism and confirmation, but I use the single word here to cover both. Christian baptism is baptism 'with the Holy Spirit'.[20] 'By one Spirit,' says St. Paul, 'we were all baptized into one body . . . and all were made to drink of the one Spirit.'[21] Baptism gives a man—or a child—open and public status and effective membership in the community of the Holy Spirit. The gift of the Spirit is not to be thought of as the sudden injection of a quasi-material power into the individual soul, but rather as the drawing of a person—or a person in the making—who has hitherto been isolated, or a member only of some sectional human society such as a family or a nation, into the universal community of persons which is knit together and vitalized by the one Spirit. Thus it is nearer the mark to speak of a man's being received into the Holy Spirit than of his receiving the Holy Spirit, who can never be a merely individual possession.

The question may be asked, and ought to be asked, whether those who have not yet been baptized are then in no sense children of God, whether Christ is not already their Head, and whether beforehand they have no part or lot in an eternal inheritance. The answer is that they are children of God, Christ is their Head, they are heirs of eternal life, for 'it was a race that Christ redeemed, and not a mere bouquet of believers'.[22] Baptism brings them into the community where these hitherto hidden truths about all men are openly acknowledged and effectively realized. It is manifest to every candid observer that the unbaptized not infrequently bring forth the fruits of the Spirit in a way that puts the baptized to shame.

In order to show what, according to Christian belief, is the effect of baptism, Father Figgis suggested as an analogy that it gives a man 'letters of naturalization in the "city which hath foundations".' [23] And while no analogy can completely meet the case, since the community of the Holy Spirit is *sui generis*, this one may be found enlightening. A man, before he becomes a naturalized citizen of the country which receives him, may have lived for many years in it and have participated in a great deal of its life. He may even have absorbed more of its tradition and have a finer sense of the privileges and duties of citizenship than many whose citizenship is already recognized and effective. All the same, naturalization decisively admits him to membership in the national community. He is then made a member of it. He can now say that the king is his king in a way that he could not before. It is no exaggeration to say that he is at that moment 'born again'.

Of the holy communion, the other sacrament of the Gospel, I will only say here that it is a rite in which the whole Gospel is expressed. It is the characteristic and corporate action of the church in which the Christians regularly come together to worship the one God and Father of all, through Jesus Christ the invisible and exalted Head of the body of which they have been made members, in the power of the Holy Spirit who unites them and enables them to worship, putting 'our desires into words which are not in our power to pray'.[24] It is an action in which the Christians look back to the work of Christ done once for all for the re-creation of the race, in which they look upward to their Head and are renewed in their dependence on him and their allegiance to him, and in which they look forward to the consummation of all things that is 'ready to be revealed at the last time'.[25]

All this, however, may seem sadly romantic when we look at the condition of the church to-day. Nevertheless, it gives us a standard or charter by which we can tell where the church has gone wrong and to what it must return, if it is not to be cast off by God as well as by men. God gave no guarantee that the church of the new covenant would respond to its calling,[26] though when it fails it has even less excuse than the church of the old covenant.

The New Testament portrays the new community of the Holy Spirit in its pristine vigour and liberty, but it does not conceal the fact that the Christians were still exposed to grave temptations and indeed that they succumbed sometimes to the grossest sins. To be brought into the community of the Spirit is not immediately to be made perfect. Far from it. The Spirit quickens into keener activity all the latent energies in a man or in a society, and so there are new possibilities of evil as well as of good. The Spirit 'wakes desires you never may forget', but he also releases powers and evokes ambitions which you have not had to handle or control before.

As the church expanded and when it had to be organized like a great institution, its temptations were both more subtle and more formidable than in the early days, and the history of the church has been darkened by all sorts of collapses and corruptions. Worst of all, and the root of all, have been lack of trust in the Holy Spirit, the Lord and Life-giver of the church, and the dependence of churchmen on other forces, and their greater attachment to a past which is obsolete than to the eternal which is always renovating. We can take note of only one or two of these failures and perversions.

In organizing itself on a large scale, which became inevitable and need not have been disastrous, the church forgot its distinctive character as a community of the Holy Spirit, and conformed to the manners and methods of political systems. Forgetting that the Holy Spirit does his healing work by persuasion and conviction, the church resorted to the weapons of coercion, which are necessary for the maintenance of political order but are incompatible with the propagation of truth. Forgetting that the living Spirit of God is its guide and governor, the church allowed those men who were entrusted with the responsibility of leadership and government under him to acquire and wield unchecked forms of power which involved their setting themselves up in his place as lords over the church. This corrosion was the more subtle in that the language of piety and the docile sentiments of the faithful could easily be exploited in the interests of the hierarchy's or the pope's will to power. Nor is it only popes and bishops who have lorded it over God's people, but priests and deacons and laymen, too.

Again, the church has often stultified its own distinguishing marks by petrifying them. Both the Word of God and the sacraments have in this way been turned to the defeat of their own purpose. Rightly used, they are the means by which the Holy Spirit keeps the church true to its charter and mission, namely, the proclamation of the Gospel throughout the world in the contemporary languages of mankind and the building up of the members of Christ in a holy community. But these means can be exalted into ends, and dead ends at that. Thus the Bible and the creeds can be treated as infallible oracles like the Koran, instead of as witnesses which the Holy Spirit will enable the church to interpret in a living way and in the light of fresh insights and discoveries. The sacraments can be treated as rites that operate impersonally and mechanically instead of in terms of personal relationship and the activity of the Holy Spirit. Sacraments can also be treated—and are being treated now—as instruments by which Christians keep themselves separate from one another, in spite of the fact that they are really witnesses to the universal scope of Christ's saving work and to the unity of mankind in the body of which he is the Head.

Nevertheless, there is a very difficult problem here, to which many are blind who cavil at the church's recalcitrance to becoming a sort of 'liberty hall' where everyone is welcome and no questions are asked. The church's attachment to traditional customs, and its refusal to conform easily to the spirit of the age and to the changing phases of human culture, are not just perverse. The church knows that it is not just a fluctuating product of historical relativity, but is a witness to the finality of God and his Law and of God's work in Christ for the race and for all ages. A vague church, or a church that applauded everybody and connived at everything, would be a futile church. 'Everything, it is now said, is more or less true; and so everyone is more or less good, and we know not under what king we are.' [27] But the church has to witness that in God there is final truth and final goodness, and that men can know under what king they are, for their King has entered into the relativities of history and has established a community in which his universal kingship is confessed and can be effectively realized. Therefore, there must always be the note of exclusion as well as of inclusion in the church.

Christian belief is irrevocably committed to the note of finality, but the mistake of the church or of sections of the church, has been to confound finality with infallibility. What is final in the church is not an inerrant Bible, nor an infallible pope, nor an irreformable system of doctrine, nor the verdict of General Councils, but the Holy Spirit who has assumed responsibility for leading men into all the truth about a final God and a final Christ. One of the works of the Holy Spirit in this age is to teach Christians to acknowledge the relativity of all systems of doctrine and forms of ecclesiastical order, so that they may be prepared to follow his guidance into such a transformation of the church as will enable it to bear to this age a witness analogous to that which the church of the apostolic age bore as it moved out faithfully, fearlessly and flexibly into the Hellenistic world.

A church thus transformed and brought into unity by the Holy Spirit will be much more like the church of the apostolic age than any of the churches that we see at present, but it will also be different from anything that has gone before. I agree with what James Martineau said a hundred years ago: 'Whatever unity may yet arise in Christendom will be no less different from any thing we have yet known than the factory from the monastery, the locomotive from the packhorse, or the *Times* newspaper from the illuminated manuscript.' [28]

If a man looks closely into what is already happening in the church or the churches, he may find signs of the beginning of this transformation, though not signs enough to give him much confidence that it will be carried through on the scale and with the speed that are required. That confidence can arise only from the conviction that the church is still in the hands of the Holy Spirit who now and for ever is its Lord and Life-giver in reality as well as in name.

NOTES

[1] See p. 15 *supra*.

[2] N. Micklem, *The Creed of a Christian*, p. 146.

[3] See Stephen Paget, *Henry Scott Holland*, p. 66.

[4] *The Bible To-day*, pp. 7f.

[5] Genesis 9:8. See also the Book of Jonah.

[6] See p. 62 *supra*.

[7] Cp. G. S. Duncan, *Jesus, Son of Man*, pp. 232f.

[8] Mark 14:23f.

[9] P. T. Forsyth, *The Church and the Sacraments*, p. 32.

[10] 1 Corinthians 15:28.

[11] This expression is taken from the bidding prayer in the 55th Canon of the Church of England. The Greek word for 'church', viz. *ecclesia*, may also be used of the whole redeemed community in heaven and on earth; see Hebrews 12:23.

[12] *Spirit of Prayer*, p. 57.

[13] Op. cit., p. 15.

[14] Op cit., p. 74.

[15] See the XIXth Article of the Church of England.

[16] Romans 10:14.

[17] 2 Corinthians 11:4; cp. Galatians 1:9.

[18] Forsyth, op. cit., p. 45.

[19] *Christus Veritas*, p. 162.

[20] Mark 1:8.

[21] 1 Corinthians 12:13.

[22] Forsyth, op. cit., p. 40.

[23] In *The Meaning of the Creed*, edited by G. K. A. Bell, p. 198.

[24] Romans 8:26 (Basic English). The R.V. has 'with groanings that cannot be uttered'; the R.S.V., 'with sighs too deep for words'.

[25] 1 Peter 1:5.

[26] It is improbable that Matthew 16:18, 'The gates of Hades shall not prevail against it', which is often taken to mean that the powers of evil shall not prevail against the church on earth, really bears this meaning. See A. McNeile, *The Gospel according to St. Matthew*, ad loc.

[27] Forsyth, op. cit., p. 151.

[28] *Miscellanies*, p. 330.

VI

THE FORGIVENESS OF SINS

*

I T has been said that, if the essence of Christian belief could be summed up in one brief phrase, it might be, 'I believe in God who forgives sins through Jesus Christ'. It is quite true that 'the forgiveness of sins', if all that it carries with it is understood, is one of the most concise summaries of the work of Christ. The prophecy of Jeremiah about the new covenant-relationship which God would establish with his people and which the coming of Christ inaugurated, concludes with, and even culminates in, this divine promise, 'I will pardon their offences, and their sin I never will recall'.[1] Our aim in this lecture is to see what the forgiveness of sins means, and why it is so fundamental and pervasive an element in Christian belief.

'The forgiveness of sins' is not an altogether satisfactory expression. It sounds too abstract. Translated into concrete terms, it means that there is a God who forgives sinners, who restores broken personal relationships, who reconciles to himself and to one another sinful men and the members of a sinful race.

We must begin by considering what sin is, more thoroughly than we have had occasion to do yet. To hear some theological neophytes talk you might suppose that the first article of the Christian faith is, 'I believe in sin, and especially in original sin'. But the first article of the Christian faith is, 'I believe in God'. In a godless world there would be no such thing as sin, for sin arises in the personal relationship between God and men. There would be faults and there would be crimes, but not sins. A fault is a failure to live up to an ideal of human conduct that we have made for ourselves. To say 'my fault' is not the same thing as to say 'my sin' or 'my guilt'. Sin is an offence against God, not merely against a human ideal, and it makes a man guilty before God. Nor is a sin the same thing as a crime. A crime is a transgression of the law of the State. Crimes no doubt are usually sins, but not necessarily so; for a State may order a man to do something that is an offence against God, and then it would be a sin *not* to commit a crime. The Christians who were sent to concentration camps under the Nazis may have committed a crime against the State, at any rate against a *de facto* State, but they were not therefore guilty before God.

The concept of sin rests on the assumption that there is a personal holy God to whom men are personally responsible and whose will they are morally bound to obey. It rests on the assumption that God makes his will known to men in their consciences. The familiar saying that 'the voice of conscience is the voice of God' is not to be dismissed as an aphorism suitable only for the kindergarten. It must not, of course, be taken to mean that whatever any man does conscientiously can without further ado be taken to be the will of God, for men can muffle and pervert the voice of conscience. But it accurately indicates that in the working of conscience there is a personal address of God to men, a personal claim of God upon men. To give heed to conscience is to give heed to God, and not merely to our own better instincts or to social pressure or to some impersonal moral law. In the Bible law is represented in a personal way. 'God spake these words, and said, I am the Lord thy God, thou shalt have none other gods but me', and so on. The delivery of the commands of God at Mount Sinai (whatever may have actually happened there; that is covered by a cloud) is a symbol of their delivery to every man in his conscience. 'Every man's heart is a Sinai', said an old English divine.[2] Sinai also symbolizes the fact that there is in the will of God for mankind something as permanent as the everlasting hills. 'Thy righteousness is like the great mountains.' [3] Bunyan compared the ten commandments to 'great guns'.[4] It is God's voice that can still be heard in them.

The commands of God are not arbitrary dictates. He does not tell men to do this or that without rhyme or reason. The Law of God for man, as it has gradually been made known, is the revelation of the way of life for which man is created, for which, being what God made him, he is fitted, and in which alone he can attain to his end. The word 'end', which is in itself ambiguous, means in this context not termination, the point at which a thing ceases to be, but fulfilment or completion of purpose—that state in which a person reaches final satisfaction and ceases to be restless.

The end of mankind in this sense is to become a community of persons in freely-willed and complete dependence on, and harmony with, the All-Holy God. All the intimations of right and wrong that God gives to men in their consciences are pointers to that end or tugs in that direction. They are God calling or drawing men towards their true end and away from false or illusory ends.

I said that in the Bible the Law of God, the communication of God's will to men, is represented in a personal way. This becomes most evident when you perceive that at last Christ himself is the Law of God for man. In Christ God finally communicated his will to men and brought man's end fully into the light—not only in Christ's teaching but in his Person, in all that he was and did. Christ did not only talk about the way, the truth and the life; he was the way, the truth and the life. He was the true Man, the normal Man, Man at last attaining his true end, perfectly responsive and obedient to the will of God. And he came to draw all men into a responsive and obedient community. Christ fulfilled the Law of God in that he fully manifested the way of life that is God's will and purpose for mankind. All God's earlier intimations, in conscience and through the prophets, of the right way of living were gathered up and crowned in Christ himself, who is the Word of God become man. God's Law is part of his Word; without it there would be no Gospel or good news.

Old writers used to illustrate Christ's fulfilling of the Law of God by the analogies of a vessel that had some water in it before but is now filled up to the brim, and of a picture that is first drawn roughly, the limbs only or lineaments, with a charcoal, but when the hand of the painter comes to draw it in colours to the life, then it is said to be filled up.[5] So Christ filled in the picture of God's will for mankind.

Whatever be the best analogy for Christ's embodying in a completely personal way God's Word to man, what men did to him and how they reacted to him revealed something else. When he first encountered his contemporaries, they seem to have been attracted and even fascinated; but when it came to the point—when the nature and extent of God's demand that he brought home to them was unfolded—men could not stand him, and they made away with him. 'Away with him, away with him!' they all cried out together.[6] Why? The answer that Christians give is—sin; not just so many particular sins that caused the crucifixion, but sin.

We must not confuse sins with sin; at least we must see how the former spring from the latter. Sins are separate acts, or words, or thoughts, each of which is a rejection of God's will and so a rebellion against him. But these separate acts spring from one root and are symptoms of the same disease, which I have called egocentricity or egotism. Selfishness is a more familiar word, but just because it is so familiar its force has been weakened. Egotism is the root human sin. It means that every man wills to make himself the centre of the world, and is inclined to judge everything with reference to his own interests. You can test that statement by observing how other people first react when a proposition is made to them. It is less pleasant, but more salutary and also more difficult, to observe one's own reactions.

The ways of egotism are exceedingly subtle. Egotism is a skilful hypocrite; it is an adept at wearing the cloak of altruism and of piety. It can persuade a man that what he wants to do for his own gratification will be of singular benefit to mankind. It can also conceal from men their weaknesses by making them lean on the approval of their party or of those who are hopelessly partial to them. A story is told of Archbishop Frederick Temple that he was once interviewing a young clergyman who, he happened to know, was engaged to a young lady in the parish where he was working. The Archbishop was taking the hapless curate to task for the poor quality of his sermons of which he had copious and reliable evidence. 'Oh!' said the young man, 'but they tell me my sermons are very good.' 'Did she?' the Archbishop sardonically inquired; and that was that.

It is not only bad men who are infected with egotism, but good men too. There were very good men among those who drove Jesus to his death. The perversity of egotism comes out in its capacity to make humble men proud of their humility and virtuous men jealous of virtue in others and righteous men self-righteous. Egotism is a canker in the human soul. It is the root of man's rebellion against God and of his refusal to live in dependence on God and in real community with other persons.

It needed the coming of Christ, the Man entirely free from egotism, to show it up. He revealed the depth and range of human sin, and condemned it for what it is—man's NO to God. As it has been put, 'Sin is condemned in the cross because it there is permitted fully to expose its true nature. Once for all it is forced into the light. What sin really is—its rebellion, malignancy, and horror—could never be completely detected or revealed while it was being committed against those who themselves shared the imperfection of the sinner.' [7]

That is why, ever since Christ's coming, men have found their rebellion against God—their egotism which expresses itself in pride or complacency or callous indifference (I couldn't care less) as well as in the grosser and more obvious sins—men have found their sinfulness most clearly and decisively exposed when Christ and above all Christ's cross is brought home to their imaginations. Then they see their own secret selves staring out at them in the face of the rigorous and self-righteous Pharisee, or in the lax and wordly Sadducee, or in the treachery of Judas betraying the best he knew, or in the denial of Peter forsaking that to which he owed everything. It is when a man sees himself there as an agent in the passion of the Lord that he is convicted of sin, and mild talk about faults and failings fades from his lips. Then a man realizes his hideous ingratitude to God and the guilt of his rebellion. Then a man realizes that he has done something to his original relation to God which he is himself entirely incapable of repairing or putting right.

There are some theologians who teach that human nature is 'totally corrupt' or 'totally depraved'. These are not expressions that occur in the Bible or the creeds. On their face they seem to say that men are absolutely sinful and incapable of doing any good at all, which is absurd, for even in the most depraved human beings we can think of, such as Titus Oates or Richard Piggott, there were some faint traces of good. But I understand that the theologians who use these expressions do not mean that. They mean that sin infects every part of man's being so that he is incapable of doing anything that is perfect or pleasing to God, for only what is perfect can be pleasing to God. 'A sinner', writes Brunner, 'is not a human being who has sinned a certain number

of times; he is a human being who sins whatever he is doing.'[8]
Richard Hooker made the point more delicately when he said,
'The best things we do have somewhat in them to be pardoned.' [9]
But it is only as men's consciences are illuminated by the Holy
Spirit in the light of Christ that they come to see how profoundly
egocentric they are, and how even their best achievements and
their best selves are infected by sin. Thus growth in the life of the
Spirit brings with it a deepening consciousness of sinfulness and
of the need for the forgiveness of sin. This is shown by the testimony of the saints, and indeed it is a commonplace of mature
Christian experience. When a man like St. Paul said, 'Christ Jesus
came into the world to save sinners. And I am the foremost of
sinners',[10] this was not mock modesty or the affected rhetoric of a
pulpiteer, but the quite sincere confession of a man who, because
he had seen so much further than other men into the holiness of
Christ, had also seen much further into his own sinfulness.

When a man is exposed to the encounter of God in Christ, he
finds himself in the first place convicted of sin. Until that is recognized, it is impossible to see why forgiveness plays so crucial a
part in Christian belief and in Christian experience. What then is
the meaning of forgiveness? How does God deal with sinful men?
What is it that God has done for men in Christ, that they could
never do for themselves, to bring them back into a relationship of
obedience and love? A French critic has said that English-speaking
theologians are *intarissables* (inexhaustible) on the question of the
atonement.[11] And it may be true that English theological literature
has been occupied with this subject out of proportion to other
doctrines of the creed. I must confess that I always find books on
the atonement—and we have some great books[12]—unsatisfying.
They usually try to explain what God has done for man in Christ
by drawing on various analogies in the relations between human
beings.

A man can suffer for other men, sacrifice himself for them;
men can forgive one another, and so on. Since men can do these
things for one another, shall we not discover, if we reflect upon
what is involved in these personal actions, what God has done for
men in Christ? But shall we? Certainly this is more promising
than to think of the atonement as a legal transaction. But is not the

relationship of God to men unparalleled or *sui generis*, and must not all analogies drawn from intra-human relationships be hopelessly inadequate? It has for this reason been proposed that we ought to try to look at the atonement from the standpoint of God, and not of man.[13] But, if this is anything more than a truism, it is impossible advice. It is like asking us to jump out of our skins and to take our seat in the celestial council chamber. Theologians do sometimes talk as though they had accomplished that presumptuous and impossible feat. The truth is that we have to do the best we can with human analogies, remembering always that they are only analogies, and that any analogy if pressed hard enough yields poison.

It must also be borne in mind that, if the atonement—God's reconciliation of this disordered and rebellious world to himself in Christ—is a fact, it is the greatest mystery that there is, and that we cannot expect to comprehend it entirely. 'About the manner of the Atonement,' wrote Dr. Hort, 'we must all feel that it lies in a region into which we can have only glimpses, and that all figures taken from things below are of necessity partial and imperfect. It is the vain attempt to bring the Divine truth down to the level of our own understandings that has created all the dark perversions of the Atonement which have justly offended sensitive consciences, and so given occasion to the denial of the truth itself.'[14]

It is sometimes said that, since no orthodox theory of the atonement has ever been defined, it is enough to affirm the fact of the atonement and there is no need to theorize about it. If that means that Christian faith means personal acceptance of Christ as the Saviour from sin, and not assent to some doctrine of the atonement, it is a wholesome reminder of what, when men start theologizing or setting themselves up as arbiters of orthodoxy, they are liable to forget. But we are bound to use our intelligence as far as we can to understand what the fact is. It may be that the most explanation can hope to do here is to remove misconceptions and to point in the direction where the truth will be found. In the case of the atonement, above all, a man has to discover the truth for himself in personal experience.

We shall do well, after all, to start from the analogy of forgiveness in human relationships. Forgiveness in human relationships has been defined as 'an active process in the mind and temper of a wronged person, by means of which he abolishes a moral hindrance to fellowship with the wrongdoer, and re-establishes the freedom and happiness of friendship.' [15] The need for divine forgiveness presupposes that the sin of a man not only injures himself and not only injures other persons, but injures God. Christian men glimpse something of what that injury is in the passion of Christ. But the passion of Christ reveals not only the effect of sin, the sin of the whole world, on God; it reveals also God's love for mankind in spite of what sin has done to him and to his world. It is an action in which God declares not merely that he is ready to forgive in so far as men will repent and amend their ways, but that, without waiting for men to repent, he has wrought a deed of reconciliation that creates a new situation between himself and mankind which makes effective repentance and amendment possible. God has entered right into the tangle and frustration and tragedy of human existence and not only *said* something, but has *done* something there to change all its possibilities. 'The Cross was not shown in the air, but inserted in the tissue of history, with the eloquence and action of affairs.' [16]

'The feeble gospel preaches "God is ready to forgive",' it has been said, 'the mighty gospel preaches "God has redeemed".' [17] God's act in Christ changes the whole race's relation to God. But, it may reasonably be asked, had not God been a forgiving God before Christ came and was crucified? Does not the Old Testament bear witness to his forgiveness? Yes, it does. But it was never before so brought home to men that God is not only, so to speak, of a forgiving disposition, but that he is actually present among men and within history with power to forgive and to make his forgiveness effective. He does not only promise pardon, but here and now he restores the relationship that sin had broken. Remember the astonishment and the scandal that Jesus caused by proclaiming to men and women that their sins actually were forgiven. 'My son, your sins are forgiven,' he said. 'It is blasphemy!' said the scribes. 'Who can forgive sins but God alone?' [18]

But, it may then be asked, if the Son of Man had authority to forgive sins during his ministry on earth, what need was there of his passion and cross to effect atonement? Is not the crucifixion in this case superfluous? How can the forgiveness of sins depend upon the cross? In line with this is the question: Is not the parable of the prodigal son the conclusive proclamation of the free divine forgiveness of sinners? And there is no mention of the cross in that. The parable of the prodigal son is ineffaceable testimony to God's readiness to forgive sinners who return to him and to receive them back; and that is its point. But it does not follow that the whole gospel of divine forgiveness is included in this parable. If it were, it would be passing strange that the apostles never seem to have used it in their preaching. Is it really meant that when Jesus had uttered the parable of the prodigal son, he might as well have considered that his work was done and have returned to heaven?[19]

Jesus came to do much more than to enlarge men's ideas of the divine forgiveness by a sublime parable. And he came to do much more than to carry the divine forgiveness into effect for the men and women whom he encountered during his ministry on earth. He came to make divine forgiveness and reconciliation effective for the race and on the scale of the world. It is his death on the cross with his resurrection and the outpouring of the Holy Spirit that has brought home to all subsequent ages and all over the world God's forgiveness and power to reconcile.

Return now to the analogy of human forgiveness. Suppose that a man has injured one of his friends by an act of meanness or treachery or deceit, so that an inevitable barrier has come between them which only the injured man can overcome. It will be much if the wrongdoer is assured in a general way that his friend is a man of a forgiving disposition. It will be more if his friend sends a messenger to him to say that though terribly wounded he is ready to forgive. It will be more still if the friend comes himself and declares that he forgives. But even human forgiveness can go to greater lengths than that, and the forgiveness that recreates personal relationships does go to greater lengths. For the friend can do something at a great cost to himself, even to giving his life, which makes a new man of the wrongdoer, raising him from a condition of abject shame to wondering gratitude, so creating a new relationship that almost puts the former friendship in the shade. That is the kind of thing that God did for mankind and to mankind in

G

Christ's cross; by his death and resurrection a new relationship was created which was henceforth open to all men.

Observe that forgiveness is not negative only. It is not like the wiping of a slate. God anyhow does not do barely negative things. Nor does forgiveness mean letting off punishment. That is a popular fallacy. Forgiveness deals with guilt not with punishment. The forgiven man cannot undo all the consequences of his sin, nor can God conjure them away with a magic wand, nor does the man want to be let off lightly. What he wants to know is that he is restored to the trust and love which he had forfeited and spurned. And if beyond this he can be shown that there is a creative power of love at work which can heal and restore not only himself but all those other human beings, known to him and unknown, whom he has injured, then he will gladly bear whatever penalties must fall upon himself.

Here is just one, necessarily inadequate, illustration from human relationships of God's way of forgiving. A tradesman in a certain town found that one of his trusted men had been systematically stealing from his warehouse for years. Some people might have been soft and let him off the punishment, which is a kind of indulgence that modern men profess to admire though they seldom practise it themselves. Other people would have been hard-boiled and would have cast the culprit adrift. But this man's employer did neither the one nor the other. He let him be tried and sentenced and sent to prison. But when the man came out of prison his employer was there to greet him with the words, 'Your place is open for you; come back; we will start afresh.' And when the man reached home, he found that his wages had been paid in full to his wife all the time he had been in prison. He was punished; but he was forgiven, and creatively forgiven. The forgiveness of God is like that.

I have been emphasizing so far the personal aspect of human sin and of God's forgiveness—the forgiveness of the individual person and his restoration to communion with God; and that is the point at which the experience of forgiveness becomes most definite and its effects are most plainly realized. But the work of Christ was to bring into being a new community in which persons are continually being reconciled both to God and to one another, and are bound together in a new kind of fellowship. This is the community of the Holy Spirit.

Christ's passion and resurrection created a community of persons who were not only individually restored and raised to a new kind of communion with God, but who were thereby brought into a new relationship with their fellows, a relationship in which they were learning that God's forgiveness both requires and enables them to forgive one another. This was a persistent note in Christ's teaching; for instance, in the Lord's Prayer, 'Forgive us our trespasses, as we forgive them that trespass against us', and in his answer to Peter, when he asked, 'Lord, how often shall my brother sin against me, and I forgive him? As many as seven times?' Jesus said to him, 'I do not say to you seven times, but seventy times seven.' [20]

Active forgiveness, forgiveness that takes the initiative, is not only a condition of the restoration of broken personal relationships, but is itself creative of new personal relationships. God forgives this man and that man, so that in the power of the Holy Spirit they may become agents of Christ's reconciling work in the world. To be forgiven and reconciled to God is not a privilege for favoured individuals. It is to be brought into a forgiven and reconciled community that is not turned in upon itself as though it could rest content with a peculiar privilege, but that is turned outward to the world of estranged and warring individuals and groups and parties. The community of the Holy Spirit is determined to bring home to all men the good news that there is pardon and reconciliation for all in the body of Christ. That is its *raison d'être*. Where a church is alive and not dead, it is moved by gratitude for forgiveness and reconciliation received to go out and extend these blessings universally; for it knows that, since the work of the Head of the body is to reconcile the world to God, this must also be the work of his members. And it is in the atmosphere of a community which lives by God's forgiveness that others who know it not can be brought to experience it. I mean, the atmosphere of a community which not only preaches but practises forgiveness and reconciliation, a community which not only passes charitable resolutions but does the works of brotherly love wherever men are in need.

We have still to look at the patent fact that the forgiveness of sin does not at once result in the abolition of sin. There are indeed some passages in the New Testament which seem to say that the acceptance of Christ as Lord and Saviour and the imparting of the Holy Spirit do raise believers immediately to a state of perfect holiness. 'How can we who died to sin still live in it?' asked St. Paul. 'You must consider yourselves dead to sin and alive to God in Christ Jesus,' he said.[21] And in the first Epistle of St. John we read: 'No one who abides in him sins; no one who sins has either seen him or known him. . . . No one born of God commits sin; for God's nature abides in him, and he cannot sin because he is born of God.'[22] But these passages are exceptional, and when they are studied in their context it is clear that they do not claim that it is possible to attain to a state of sinless perfection in this world.[23]

These sayings and others like them spring out of that experience of sudden transformation and spiritual power which was characteristic of the apostolic age and which recurs in every great spiritual revival. But the New Testament as a whole leaves its readers in no doubt that the forgiven sinners, however transformed, are still sinners. 'If we say that we have no sin we deceive ourselves'—the words come from the same Epistle of St. John (1:8). It was only the first-fruits of the Spirit that even the apostles claimed to have received.

This leads to the distinction that has been drawn in traditional Christian doctrine, especially since the Reformation, between man's 'justification' and his 'sanctification'. These are both New Testament terms, though they are not the only terms, and not necessarily the best terms, in which the truth of man's reconciliation to God can be stated. These particular terms have, however, played so important a part in the theology of the West that one needs to know what they mean, even if one considers that in future other terms might with advantage be used in their stead. As I said, they are New Testament words, but in the New Testament they are not used with the consistency and precision to which systematic theologians aspire. Vast works of controversial divinity have been devoted to this subject. It was one of the crucial theological questions upon which the Reformation turned, and it is far from being only of historical interest. Here I can enter only into its rudiments, and for the layman they may well suffice.

The question at stake is, How can sinful man get right with God? Can he put himself right by amending his ways and by doing good works, works that will be well-pleasing to God, and so gain his favour? But that is just what sinful man cannot do, however hard he tries, not even if he is an Anglo-Saxon who is confident that men can be justified only by what they do themselves. The doctrine of justification by faith means that man, who cannot put himself right with God by any works that he can do, is nevertheless put right by the work of Christ. He is justified, that is to say, not by any righteousness that he can achieve by his own laborious efforts, but by the righteousness of Christ. Christ is the New Man, who has offered himself up to the Father not merely as a substitute for sinful men, but as the source and spring of a new human righteousness which is available for mankind and which can be imparted to all men in the community of the Holy Spirit. On man's side the means by which this new God-given righteousness is received is 'faith', which is itself the gift of the Holy Spirit. Faith means a man's putting his whole trust and confidence not in anything he can do or earn, but in Christ the Head of the new creation, the Reconciler of the world and the source of all righteousness. 'It is only because God does everything that man can do something, not as price but in gratitude.'[24]

To be justified by faith does not mean that a man, by the act of putting his whole confidence in the righteousness of Christ, is thereby at once made wholly righteous in himself, or is completely freed from sin. It means that henceforth the basis of his life and the ground of his confidence have been changed. He no longer strives to get into God's good books by cultivating and accumulating virtue in himself. He has once for all called the bluff of Mr. Bernard Shaw's dictum, 'Forgiveness is a beggar's refuge; we must pay our debts.'[25] He has confessed that he is a beggar, and that he cannot pay his debts to God. But he knows that, bankrupt as he is in himself, he has a standing with God in Christ his Head. He has no righteousness in himself, but in Christ he has been made an heir of all righteousness, and the Holy Spirit will enable him gradually to grow up into the righteousness of Christ. Hence the motive of his obedience to God is no longer the hope of acquiring merit or of putting himself right or of paying his debts, but thanksgiving to God who freely and gratuitously sets him right in Christ while he is still a sinner in himself.

Sanctification is the name that has been given to the process by which the man who receives his justification by faith in Christ is gradually transformed into the likeness of Christ and enabled to bring forth the fruits of the Spirit—'love, joy, peace, patience, kindness, goodness, faithfulness, gentleness, self-control'.[26] This process is not completed in this life, not even in the greatest saints. The Christian man can never sit back and say, 'Now I have attained to my end; now I am completely sanctified.' He has no ground for pride or self-conceit. For as he advances in sanctification, the Holy Spirit shows him more and more of the depths and completeness of the holiness to which he is called, and therefore he becomes aware of sins which he had not perceived before. Thus you have the paradoxical result, which I have already pointed out, that growth in holiness is also growth in awareness of sin and in penitence. The man who is justified by faith and who is being sanctified by the Holy Spirit realizes increasingly how entirely he depends on the righteousness of Christ and on the forgiveness of sins.

But the process of sanctification is not automatic or inevitable. In fact, it is possible for it to go all wrong. It is possible for a man to forget that he is justified by faith alone, and to fall into the error of supposing that the work of the Holy Spirit in him is his own work and to become secretly proud. It is possible for a man to make the righteousness of Christ which is being imparted to him a ground of self-righteousness. It is possible for him to fall back into regarding the good works, which he is bound and enabled to do, as a means of acquiring merit or of earning a reward, instead of as a hopelessly inadequate offering of gratitude to God who has done everything for him in Christ. And then he is back in the old bondage from which Christ and his apostles proclaimed man's deliverance, the bondage of legalism. The legalists, the men who design to put themselves right with God by compliance with a code of moral or religious conduct, are not bad men, but good men,[27] whose goodness is ruined because they do not live in daily recognition of the fact that they are justified by faith alone, that is, by Christ's righteousness and not by their own. Legalists do not know the glorious liberty of the children of God—the freedom that Christ brings from anxiety and fussiness and scrupulosity.

It is the relapse into legalism that can make a very religious man unlovely in himself (despite all his piety and devotion), censorious of his neighbours,[28] and a caricature of godliness. Not only individuals but churches that fail to base their doctrine and discipline on 'justification by faith' become involved again in that elaborate legalism from which the Gospel of Jesus Christ delivered the church of the old covenant. The church of the new covenant forgets its charter when it forgets that it exists, not to advocate a new technique of being good or religious, but to enable men to live in the light and strength, in the charity and humility, of the forgiveness of sins.

Thus the doctrine of justification by faith is a very wholesome doctrine. Nevertheless, observe in conclusion that men are brought into that personal relationship with God which is called salvation or the glorious liberty of the children of God, not by acceptance or understanding of the *doctrine* of justification by faith, but by actual faith in Christ the Justifier of mankind. Multitudes of men and women who could never mouth the doctrine, still less follow the intricate disputations of theologians about it, or even the quite rudimentary account of it that I have just tried to give, have in fact been justified by faith and have known what it is to thank God daily for the forgiveness of sins.

NOTES

[1] Jeremiah 31:34.
[2] Joseph Hall, *Works*, 1837 edition, 1:109.
[3] Psalm 36:6.
[4] See S. T. Coleridge, *Notes on English Divines*, 1:335.
[5] See Henry Hammond, *A Practical Catechism*, Book II, Section iii.
[6] Luke 22:18; John 19:15.
[7] H. R. Mackintosh, *The Christian Experience of Forgiveness*, p. 198.
[8] *The Mediator*, p. 142.
[9] *Sermons*, edited Keble, iii. 493.
[10] I Timothy, 1:15.
[11] A. Loisy, *Mémoires*, ii. 327.
[12] E.g. McLeod Campbell, *The Nature of the Atonement*; R. C. Moberly, *Atonement and Personality*. Principal Denney held that Campbell's book was the only classical theological book that had come from Scotland. See his *Letters to W. Robertson Nicoll*, p. xx.
[13] See H. W. Clark, *The Cross and the Eternal Order*.
[14] *Life and Letters of F. J. A. Hort*, ii. 157.
[15] Mackintosh, op. cit., p. 28.
[16] P. T. Forsyth, *The Christian Ethic of War*, p. 170.
[17] P. T. Forsyth, *The Cruciality of the Cross*, p. 52.
[18] Mark 2:5ff.
[19] Cp. P. T. Forsyth, *The Work of Christ*, p. 106.
[20] Matthew 18:21f.
[21] Romans 6:2, 11.
[22] I John 3:6, 9.
[23] See Vincent Taylor, *Forgiveness and Reconciliation*, pp. 159–165.
[24] Mackintosh, op. cit., p. 108..
[25] Quoted by J. N. Figgis, *The Gospel and Human Needs*, p. 108.
[26] Galatians 5:22f.
[27] 'Moralistic legalism—Pharisaism of every kind, constitutes on the one hand the place of greatest nearness of God; and on the other the place of greatest distance from God.'—E. Brunner, *The Divine Imperative*, p. 64.
[28] 'The final proof of the genuine spirit of humility in the "elect", of their "brokenness of spirit", is their capacity for mercy and forgiveness. Without consciousness of their own need of forgiveness, "good" people never show mercy towards "bad" people.'—Reinhold Niebuhr, *Human Destiny*, p. 20.

VII

ETERNAL LIFE

★

PRINCIPAL DENNEY, the eminent Scots divine, once wrote to a friend describing in outline the subjects of a course of lectures that he was going to deliver in the United States, and he concluded with these words, 'Also I wish to say something on Eschatology'.[1] I flatter myself that in this course of lectures I have so far avoided the use of the word 'eschatology', though this is not to say that I have avoided, or wished to avoid, what the word connotes. If you start reading contemporary theology, or if you listen to the conversation of theological students, you will find that 'eschatology' is at present a very fashionable word. It is therefore desirable to know what it means, and whether it stands for so important an element in Christian belief as the present frequency of its employment is calculated to suggest.

The Greek word *eschata* means 'last things', and the dictionary definition of the English word 'eschatology' is 'the science of the four last things: death, judgment, heaven, and hell'.[2] A treatment of these four last things was an accepted part of traditional Christian doctrine, and the last section of any systematic work on Christian dogma was devoted to them. When I was a young clergyman it was still the convention in many churches to preach a course of sermons on the four Sundays in the season of Advent on death, judgment, heaven, and hell. And there was a pretty conventional, and I should say somewhat arid, way of handling these topics. Neither the preacher nor his auditory found the subject very exciting, for the lurid descriptions of hell-fire, which had been a feature of the pulpit oratory of earlier generations, had been refined away.

The present vogue of the word 'eschatology' is not the result of preachers' infusing fresh life into their Advent sermons. It is in the lecture-room and the study, rather than in the pulpit and the pew, that eschatology has come alive and absorbed attention, and it has done so for two reasons: on the one hand, as a consequence of fresh ways of interpreting the New Testament; and on the other, from a desire to discover whether Christian belief about the last things illuminates man's understanding of history, especially the history of these tumultuous times.

About the beginning of this century a bombshell was dropped into the placid fields of New Testament study by some scholars on the continent—notably, Alfred Loisy, Johannes Weiss and Albert Schweitzer. By English writers and students the last of these, Schweitzer, is usually credited—or discredited—with having dropped the bomb single-handed, but that is because it was the translation into English of a book of his—*The Quest of the Historical Jesus* (1910)—that first made English readers aware of what had happened. Schweitzer was not, in fact, the sole author of what came to be called the 'eschatological' interpretation of the New Testament.

No one who studies the New Testament closely can fail to observe that words are attributed to the apostles, and indeed to Jesus himself, which imply that they expected that the world was shortly coming to an end, and that there would be a final cataclysm which would usher in the return of Christ, the last judgment, and the consummation of the kingdom of God or of God's kingly rule over his people. In the nineteenth century scholars had not been blind to this feature of the New Testament, but they had been embarrassed by it. They had wanted to find that Christian belief, particularly belief in Christ, was consistent with the general ideas of evolution and historical development and with the hope of social progress. The eschatological (or, as they are also called, 'apocalyptic') elements in the New Testament did not fit in with the assumptions and aspirations of that peaceful and progressive period. The tendency therefore was for the eschatological elements in the New Testament to be explained as the husk in which the faith and message of the apostles were at first enclosed—a husk soon broken and forgotten leaving the kernel to do its fruitful work. As regards the words attributed to Jesus himself which anticipated the impending end of the world, these were explained by the theory either that they had been retrospectively and mistakenly put into his mouth by the early

Christians or that he had accommodated himself to a current idiom which he had not really taken seriously himself.

The bombshell, of which I have spoken, consisted in the assertion, learnedly argued and persuasively presented, that not only the apostles but Jesus himself had taken perfectly seriously the expectation of the near end of the world and the arrival of the last things, indeed that this was the heart of their message which gave it its driving force. It was suggested that the discovery of evolutionary or progressive ideas in the New Testament was merely the reading back into it of ideas which nineteenth century minds wished to find there, but which were not there in fact. The theologians who in that way attempted to modernize the figure of Jesus were ingeniously compared to a man who looks down a deep well and sees his own reflection at the bottom.

Subsequent study has in various ways modified the thoroughgoing eschatological interpretation of the New Testament, especially as it was put forward by Schweitzer whose manner of dealing with the documents was in some respects arbitrary and cavalier. But the bomb has made a permanent difference and things can never be the same again.

The most interesting, and at present the most popular, recasting of the eschatological interpretation of the New Testament is the theory of what is called 'realized eschatology', which is associated with the name of Professor C. H. Dodd. According to this, it is quite true that the apostles and Jesus himself proclaimed the arrival of the last things and the coming of the kingdom of God. But what they meant, or rather what Jesus himself meant, even though the apostles to some extent misunderstood him, was not that these things were going to happen in the near future, but that they had happened already, or at any rate had begun to happen. In the coming of Christ and especially in the events in which his coming culminated, the end of the world or the last things had entered into history. In his life, death, and resurrection, and by the outpouring of the Holy Spirit, the kingdom of God actually became incorporated, so to speak, in the process of history. Jesus was not the herald of a future kingdom of God, but in his Person the kingdom of God was really present, confronting and calling men. To respond to him and to receive the Holy

Spirit was to begin living in the kingdom of God at once, and not only to look forward to it as a promise to be fulfilled in the future.

The new age, the world to come, which had been the burden of prophecy and apocalypse, had arrived and had supervened upon the old world where change and sin and death still operated. The two worlds overlapped; to be a Christian was to be living in two worlds at once. The last things were realized even while the old world went on. Hence the name by which this view of the matter is known, 'realized eschatology'.

This school of theology makes much of the word 'crisis' or judgment. The coming of the last things in Christ, the intersection of time by eternity, exposed the sinfulness of the old world, and was a divine judgment upon it.   But it was also an act of divine mercy, enabling those who accepted the judgment and who believed in Christ to receive God's forgiveness and to enter into the new creation while still living in the old world. This way of interpreting the New Testament, in the dialectical terms of judgment and mercy, is held to offer a clue to the meaning of every subsequent crisis in history. Every crisis in history, if we interpret it aright, will be found to register God's judgment on the corruption of the world and his offer of reconciliation and a new beginning to all who turn to him and repent. Anyhow, it is in terms such as these that the New Testament is nowadays being discussed and expounded in our theological schools, and this circumstance is palpably one of the factors that accounts for the vogue of the word 'eschatology'.

But I said there was also another factor, namely a desire to discover whether Christian belief about the last things illuminates man's understanding of history, especially the history of these tumultuous times. That is to say, a man may be driven to eschatology not only by the New Testament, but also by the newspapers. About this second factor I need say less because it is obvious and familiar enough. Roughly speaking, before 1914 the idea of progress provided considering men with a working philosophy of history and with an impetus to the exercise of social and political responsibility. The catastrophic events that have taken place since then, the increasing sense of insecurity and bewilderment, have changed the climate of thought, and have invited a theology which takes a less sanguine view of historical development and which speaks more prominently of an other-worldly hope. Thus a strongly eschatological interpretation of Christian belief has found favourable soil and has had a congenial environment. It is not surprising that it has become fashionable among those who are sensitive to the signs of the times.

That is by way of introduction to the subject of this lecture. I am not going to elaborate the theme of 'realized eschatology' in so many words. In so far as it seems to me to have unearthed what is true and important in the New Testament, I have taken its findings into account in the preceding lectures, and shall do so in this one. Before proceeding to speak about Christian belief concerning the end of the world, immortality and resurrection, and eternal life, I would only add a word of warning about a danger which attends the eschatological theology that is at present fashionable. It has the unhappy effect of encouraging in its adepts the use of an imposing jargon which often conceals confused and incoherent thinking, and gives rise to the illusion that a man has said something very profound when all he has done in fact, is to have uttered some strange, long words. This kind of self-deception is not, of course, peculiar to eschatological (or crisis or dialectical) theology or to theology at all; it is a very common human failing. Carlyle once described some lectures by Emerson as 'moonshine' and 'intellectual sonatas'. If you come across theologians or theological students whom you suspect of talking in that style, you will be doing us a good service if you press us very hard to explain exactly what we mean.

And now for Christian belief about the end of the world. I have called attention already to the ambiguity of the word 'end'.[3] It may mean either that which is last in time or that which completes a process by bringing its purpose to fulfilment. If I am writing a book, I could mean by the 'end' of my work either the moment at which I concluded my correction of the final proofs by inserting or deleting a comma, or I could mean the whole purpose for which I wrote the book, which was present to my mind and influencing my work throughout, but which could begin to take its complete effect only after the book was ended in the former sense.

If we are considering the end of the world or of the universe or of history, the notion of a last moment in time is self-contradictory. For, if we think of it as happening in time, we must go on to think of a time when it will have happened, and therefore of something coming after it.[4] On the other hand, the notion of an unending series of events is equally unthinkable, so that we are here faced with a dilemma with which the human mind cannot cope. But fortunately it is not urgently necessary that we should be able to cope with it. For if we could conceive of an event which was last in time, there is no reason to suppose that it would be of any particular importance, any more than the last comma I insert or delete in the proofs of my book.

In the other sense, however, the end of the world or the end of history is of the utmost importance; it is conceivable; it is not self-contradictory, however mysterious it may be. The question here is: In what purposed end (if any) is the whole process of history to be completed and fulfilled? So far as I can understand, Christian belief has nothing special to say about what will be last in time, nor has it any special interest in the moment at which, or the manner in which, human existence will cease on this planet. That is to say, Christian belief is equally consistent with a variety of speculations upon that point, and it does not stand or fall with any of them.

But it does stand or fall with the conviction that the process of history has a purpose which will be, and is being, completed and fulfilled. That purpose is the creation and, because of sin, the re-creation and gathering together of a community of persons who freely love God and rejoice eternally in his glory. The word 'eternal' in its current use is not only ambiguous but multiguous.[5] As I am using it here, it means neither going on for ever and ever nor simply timeless; it points to an order of being which transcends time, upon which time depends, and which cannot be adequately described either positively or negatively in temporal terms. Our minds as they exist at present are needed and designed to deal with the temporal process, and they are not qualified to comprehend the eternal. Nevertheless, man can to some extent apprehend the eternal, or get an inkling of what eternity means,[6] as for example when he comes up against what is final or absolute or overwhelmingly beautiful or what makes an unconditional demand upon him.

The purpose for which the world exists is, according to Christian belief, in this sense an eternal purpose and it will have an eternal consummation. The only way in which this purpose can be made imaginable and vivid to human minds is by the employment of ideas or pictures cast in temporal or spatial imagery, that is, by mythology. In the Person and the Work of Christ, God expressed as much of himself and of his eternal purpose as can be expressed within the historical process, so that here we have to do with a myth that is fully historical. In the coming or advent of Christ the eternal once for all became incarnate in time and, for all who believe that, time can never be the same again. That is the central conviction with which Christian belief stands or falls. But Christian belief, using the resources that the Bible supplies, also employs myths which are not historical though they make use of temporal imagery. Most conspicuously, God's purpose for the world and his relation to mankind are illuminated in the unhistorical mythology of the creation, on the one hand, and of the last judgment and second advent of Christ, on the other. We have already seen[7] that the myth of the creation is not to be understood as a transcript of what actually occurred at the beginning of time or when human existence originated on this planet. What it is really speaking about is the creative relation in which God always stands to the whole universe and to every man.

Likewise, the myth of doomsday and the final advent of Christ (sometimes called 'the Parousia') is not a forecast of what will happen at a future moment in time, but a way of conveying to mankind the relationship, in which God always stands to the race, of final judge and deliverer. 'It is evident', wrote the late Professor Quick, 'that the notions of a last day and a second advent are not to be taken literally at all.'[8] And Professor Dodd has said, 'It is impossible to think of Doomsday as a coming event in history. An occasion which gathers together at once all the generations of men who have ever lived is obviously outside the order of space and time in which history takes place. We are dealing with symbol. . . . Behind the symbolism of Doomsday (often fantastic to our minds) this is the truth: that the verdict upon history, and upon all the actors in it, is pronounced simply by confrontation with the Word of God, made flesh in Christ.' [9]

Expressions like 'the last judgment' or 'the great assize' do not mean that at a chronological end of history there will be legal proceedings on a gigantic scale, consisting of a trial and leading up to a verdict. The trial of man is proceeding now and all the time, and the facts to be tried are fully known to God as they occur. He will not need to unearth or disentangle them at some future date. The myth of the last judgment has a twofold significance. On the one hand, it means that the judge with whom in the last resort man has to reckon—a last resort which is always present—is God, and not merely the State, or social convention, or his own conscience. On the other hand, it means that divine judgment is not only an affair between God and individuals. There is a judgment of mankind. All our social relations and activities are exposed to the divine judgment. Christ is the judge as well as the redeemer of the race. There is a solidarity of mankind in sin and therefore in exposure to divine judgment, as well as in salvation from sin and in divine justification. The myth of the last judgment strikes this universal note in what otherwise might be taken individually.

According to the Bible, however, the ultimate issue of history or the end of the world is not the last judgment of mankind but the final victory of God. It is the egotism of men which has led them, when they think of the end of the world, to get lost in speculations about their own fate or the fate of others, about whether few or many or all will be saved. The Bible does nothing to encourage such speculations, although of course it bids every man take with the utmost seriousness his own standing with God. Its theme is the promised and sure triumph of God's righteousness and of his eternal purpose—the universal restoration not only of mankind but of the whole cosmos, to which he has set his hand.

Similarly, it is the egotism or self-concern of men that has led them to be preoccupied with the question of their own survival of death or with the immortality of the soul. The immortality of the soul—if it means that there is a part of every man, a kind of soul-substance, that is immortal—is not a Christian doctrine, though it has often been supposed to be and is still frequently confused with the Christian doctrine. The expression 'immortality of the soul' does not occur in the Bible or the creeds, though admittedly some theologians have made use of it. The Bible is preoccupied with God and his relation to mankind. It does not speak about any inherent capacity of the human soul to survive death. 'Many believers in God reject belief in the immortality of the soul. And on the other hand, some have believed in the immortality of the soul, while rejecting belief in God.' [10] The Bible certainly speaks of immortality; its supreme interest however is in the continuity not of individual organisms, whether physical or psychical, but of the personal relationship between God and men. The ground of its belief in immortality is not that the human soul must go on, but that life in God, and especially in the risen Christ, cannot cease.[11] 'The Christian ground for immortality', it has been well said, 'is that the Lord hath need of him',[12] and not that man wants or needs to be immortal for his own sake. The message of the Bible is not that there is 'a future state' awaiting individual souls, but that God shall be all in all in his new creation.[13]

In this connexion, it is not of the immortality of the soul but of the resurrection of the body that Christian belief, like the Bible, speaks. In God's new, immortal creation men are not ghosts; they are not disembodied spirits; they are not absorbed into an unconscious cosmic soul. They retain their personal identity, for God's purpose for them is an inheritance in which nothing will be lacking to a fully personal relationship. The work of Christ is to bring not only souls but whole men into a complete and eternal relationship with God. All that the body stands for in this world as a medium of personal expression and self-realization is to be unimaginably transformed and to receive its consummation in the world to come. Indeed the whole natural order is destined not to mere destruction, dissolution or disappearance, but to transformation. 'The creation itself will be set free from its bondage to decay and obtain the glorious liberty of the children of God.' [14]

H

Obviously, this universal transformation is inconceivable, in the sense that our minds as at present constituted cannot form any adequate conception of it. 'Language', said Professor Nairne, 'is built of images from time and space and it seems all but impossible to express in words that excursion beyond the things of sense which perhaps can be made in the dim movement of the silent mind.'[15] It is doubtful whether the biblical mythology of the new heavens and the new earth, or of the new Jerusalem 'coming down out of heaven from God, prepared as a bride adorned for her husband',[16] can be improved upon, unless the Bible itself improves upon it in the simple, pregnant and conclusive sentence, 'We shall see him as he is.'[17]

All the same, Christians have tried in crude ways to conceive the form and manner of the resurrection of the body. It has been imagined as a resuscitation of relics, as though the mortal remains of earthly bodies would be reassembled at the last day and a new body constituted out of them. There are traces of this notion in the New Testament alongside its main emphasis which is quite different. It has certainly been taken seriously in the Christian tradition. That deplorable hymn, 'On the resurrection morning Soul and body meet again' presupposes it, and it lingers still in certain funeral rites and graveyard addictions and also where you meet dogmatic objections to the practice of cremation. But apart from those melancholy legacies, Christian belief no longer confuses the resurrection of the body with a resuscitation of relics. In confessing that that confusion ought never to have been made, it is not just trying to get out of a difficulty, but is recovering the profounder insight of the New Testament into the meaning of God's new creation.

There is another point about the doctrine of the resurrection of the body, as distinguished from that of the immortality of the soul, which should not be overlooked. The word 'immortal' means not subject to death, and applied to man it must mean that there is at any rate part of a man which need not and in fact cannot die. The word 'resurrection' on the other hand presupposes the death of the whole man, every part of him. And this is in line with the whole tenour of the New Testament, for there the fact of universal death is taken seriously. 'In Adam all die.' It does not use euphemisms such as 'passing on' or 'passing over' which are popular nowadays. Death with all that it entails of separation, tragedy and mystery is a bitter necessity. The death of a man is not only natural like the death of animals or vegetables; it is also unnatural. We rebel against it.

Professor Tillich has put it thus: 'Something in us rebels against death wherever it appears. We rebel at the sight of a corpse, we rebel against the death of children, of young people, of men and women in their strength. We even feel a tragic element in the passing of old people, with their experience, wisdom, and irreplaceable individuality. We rebel against our own end, against its definitive, inescapable character. We would not rebel if death were simply natural, as we do not rebel against the falling of the leaves.'[18] Christ himself experienced this aversion as he approached the moment of death, and indeed a sense of dereliction such as no other man has known.

But the New Testament not only deals faithfully with the tragic necessity of physical death. It teaches also that there has to be a willing surrender of the whole of a man's life, of all his natural powers, in order that he may be raised to what it calls 'eternal life'. 'Whoever of you does not renounce all that he has, cannot be my disciple';[19] 'He laid down his life for us, and we ought to lay down our lives for the brethren.'[20] 'Christ has given to the idea of resurrection the quite new meaning of life restored and glorified *through and by means of* death.'[21] The human personality enters into life eternal not through some supposedly undying element in its make-up, but through a complete death and resurrection. By the death and resurrection of Christ their Head all men are enabled thus to die and to be raised to eternal life. 'We are convinced that one has died for all; therefore all have died. And he died for all, that those who live might live no longer for themselves but for him who for their sake died and was raised.'[22]

Here we reach what is at first sight, and not only at first sight, the most paradoxical assertion of the New Testament, the mystery of eternal life in the midst of time and of the risen life here and now. The church's 'paramount aim and object', said Coleridge, 'is another world, not a world *to come* exclusively, but likewise *another that now is*.'[23] That strikes the right note—or the right chord—or the right discord. In the New Testament the expression 'eternal life' is not used always in precisely the same sense, but fundamentally it means not merely 'a future life' nor 'everlasting life' (not the old kind of life prolonged for ever), but life in the new age which the coming of Christ has inaugurated. It is life in personal fellowship with God through Jesus Christ. It is the life of which the Holy Spirit is the creator and giver. It is a present and experienced reality to those who believe in Christ and who by believing come to know him and through him the Father. The force of the word 'eternal' here is not to extend the possession of life in time but to carry it into a new dimension. Eternity is to be thought of not quantitatively but qualitatively. Eternity is beyond time in the sense not of coming after it, but of being deep within it. This is another way of saying that the kingdom of God in which man is brought into that communion with God for which he was created is already present. Men can enter into it now, and live here in the light and strength of it.

Thus eternal life, according to Christian belief, is not only a hope, an expectation, or a promise of a future state. It is here and now for all who will believe and receive it. If it awaits men, it awaits their faith in it now, not in a next world. Yet it is not as simple as that, for while the world to come has already arrived, the old world continues in existence—that is, the world in which there is change and temptation and sin and death. Believers in Christ are not taken out of this world, or transported into an ivory tower whence they can regard it with complete detachment.

They are still in this world and bound up with it; they share in God's responsibility for it and will do so as long as history lasts, or as long as they live on earth. Although eternal life can be a present experience and a present possession, it cannot in history or on this side of death be a complete experience or a final possession. It is the beginning of a new kind of personal fellowship with God in the community of the Holy Spirit, which is capable of incalculable increase. Its consummation always lies beyond what is known or experienced here and now. The New Testament, in describing the Christian experience, speaks of it as 'an earnest',[24] that is a guarantee or instalment of what is yet to come. It speaks about 'tasting the powers of the age to come';[25] they can be tasted now, but only tasted. It speaks of the 'first-fruits of the Spirit';[26] the final harvest and ingathering lie in a consummation which is beyond the possibilities of present experience, and await the final restoration and transformation of all things.

Professor Nairne brought out one side of the truth when he said, 'Heaven once meant the sky; then it meant another world; now there is no other world, all life is "the Father's house".'[27] The Christian believer thankfully recognizes the truth of a saying like that. All the same, there *is* still 'another world'—the world that is at enmity with God, the egocentric world. This world still has its hold on those who believe in Christ, and it is the source of a constant tension in their existence. Emphasis on the kingdom of God and eternal life as being already present, or on all life as being now 'the Father's house', can lead men into a dangerous idealism, to a whitewashing of the dark realities of the struggle for power that is going on incessantly, even in those who imagine that they have nothing to do with it. It can deaden men's awareness of the persistence and urgency of the conflict that is ever proceeding in the world and in themselves, and in which they must take sides. It can gloss over the constant possibility of falling away from God into eternal death, which means existence out of personal fellowship with God and in defiance of him.

Eternal life is not a refuge from the storms of history or from the necessities of political decision. Still less is it an interesting problem that is up for discussion or an attractive theme for an article in a Sunday newspaper. It is not chess, but war. It is a destiny pressing upon men and claiming their daily response, but a destiny which they walk in daily peril of rejecting and losing.[28] The doctrine of a particular or individual judgment upon each man at or after death, which in the New Testament lies alongside the sense of the divine judgment of the world as a past and present reality, preserves this note of urgency and of the momentousness of decisions yet to be taken. The New Testament does not waft men into a world of timeless, mystic contemplation, but (in the words of an American writer) it makes 'men tingle, yes, even to their physical nerve tips, with the sense of an infinite hazard, a wrath to come, a heavenly city to be gained or lost in the process of time and by the use of our freedom.' [29]

What then in the end of the day, or rather at the beginning of the day and at the beginning of each day, is the decision, according to Christian belief, that men are called upon to make and to act upon? At bottom, faith is not the acceptance or reacceptance of a detailed creed nor of a system of dogma that has been worked out once for all; for in all that very much remains mysterious and unfathomed. It is personal trust in Christ, not in Christianity. It is the placing of absolute confidence in the Christ who came once for all to establish a universal kingdom and to bring back a rebellious world to the one God and Father of all—the Christ who lives and reigns for ever despite all the clouds and darkness that surround him and all the evil that still thwarts the realization of his kingly rule. He is a Christ who is still going forth conquering and to conquer, and the decision of faith is the decision to fight on his side in the small corner of the battlefield where a man finds himself and where the full and final strategy of victory may be very obscure.

'I find that my faith suffers nothing by leaving a thousand questions open, so long as I am convinced on two or three main lines,' wrote Bishop Lightfoot, a week before his death, to Archbishop Benson.[30] Convinced of the reality of the living God, Father, Son, and Holy Spirit, a man may indeed leave a thousand questions open; and that conviction, brought to a point, means staking everything on the finality of Jesus Christ, the Word of God made flesh, the Light of the world. But it remains a very dark world of which he is the light, and a Christian man need not pretend that it is otherwise. 'Be assured,' said F. W. Robertson, 'there is little to be known here; much to be borne; something to be done. What you are, and what your life means, you do not know. God only knows. You must be content with twilight except when contrast with darkness makes the twilight seem, as it really is in comparison, a blaze of light.' [31]

And for some men at any rate, who hold to their faith in Christ, the sense of the darkness as well as of the light deepens as life goes on. There is a Roman Catholic service, called *Tenebrae*, that is held in Holy Week, during which a number of candles in a triangular-shaped candlestick are one by one extinguished, till a time comes when one candle alone remains alight at the top of the candlestick while the whole of the rest of the church is in darkness. This was used by Father Tyrrell as an illustration of the point I am trying to make.

'As at Tenebrae (he wrote) one after another the lights are extinguished, till one alone—and that the highest of all—is left, so it is often with the soul and her guiding stars. In our early days these are many—parents, teachers, friends, books, authorities—but, as life goes on, one by one they fail and leave us in deepening darkness, with an increasing sense of the mystery and inexplicability of all things, till at last none but the figure of Christ stands out luminous against the prevailing night.' [32]

NOTES

[1] *Letters to W. Robertson Nicoll*, p. 4

[2] Oxford English Dictionary.

[3] See p. 88 *supra*.

[4] See O. C. Quick, *Doctrines of the Creed*, pp. 245f.

[5] See F. C. S. Schiller, *Logic for Use*, p. 420, who distinguishes and illustrates five senses of the word.

[6] See C. E. Raven, *The Creator Spirit*, pp. 205f.

[7] See p. 30 *supra*.

[8] Op. cit., p. 250.

[9] *The Bible To-day*, pp. 115f.

[10] Quick, op. cit., p. 263.

[11] See P. T. Forsyth, *This Life and the Next*, p. 23.

[12] Ibid., p. 38.

[13] Cp. A. Nairne, *The Life Eternal Here and Now*, p. 69.

[14] Romans 8:21.

[15] Nairne, op. cit., p. 39.

[16] Revelation 21:2.

[17] 1 John 3:2.

[18] *The Shaking of the Foundations*, pp. 70f.

[19] Luke 14:33.

[20] 1 John 3: 16.

[21] Quick, op. cit., p. 267.

[22] 2 Corinthians 5:14f.

[23] *Church and State*, p. 136.

[24] 2 Corinthians 1:22:5; Ephesians 1:14.

[25] Hebrews 6:5.

[26] Romans 8:23.

[27] Op. cit., p. 116.

[28] Cp. Forsyth, *This Life and the Next*, p. 59.

[29] W. E. Hocking, *The Meaning of God in Human Experience*, p. xiv.

[30] *Life of E. W. Benson*, ii. 289.

[31] *Life and Letters of F. W. Robertson*, ii. 39.

[32] See *The Soul's Orbit*, edited by M. D. Petre, p. 23; cp. *Autobiography and Life of George Tyrrell*, ii. 79–83.

INDEX

★

OTHER BOOKS BY ALEC R. VIDLER

Christian Belief and This World

This is really a sequel to *Christian Belief*

'. . . what is now needed is a basic *theology* of terrestrial values and a realistic approach to its practical implementation. To have presented both in bold outline is the outstanding achievement of this small volume.' *Times Educational Supplement*   12s 6d net

Prophecy and Papacy

A Study of Lamennais, the Church and the Revolution

'. . . the best book on Lamennais in English, perhaps in any language, and certainly one of the best studies of Church history to be written in modern times.' Christopher Sykes in *Time and Tide*   25s net

Essays in Liberality

'. . . the book as a whole may be taken as a pronouncement by a distinguished Anglican theologian about matters of contemporary importance and interest.' *Spectator*   15s net

SCM PRESS